THE TESTIMONY OF A BLACK SHEEP

Willie R. Stokes

Printed in the United States of America
ISBN pending

CONTENTS

ACKNOWLEDGMENTS

I am grateful to all for their share in this short testimony.

To Raymond Fox, minister and brother in Christ, for his wonderful input and help in editing and preparing the final copy of this testimony. I am most grateful for his weekly visits which gave me the motivation and determination to complete the finishing touches on my testimony.

To Michael Fox for his time and hardwork in helping to prepare the final draft for publication: Thank you, my brother in Christ!

To Jaime Pineda, an ex-soldier of the Mexican Mafia, and to Frank Olvera, an ex-member of the Northern Structure, for their God-given artistic talent in producing the cover. "Muchas gracias, mis Hermanos!"

DEDICATION

To all mis hermanos y hermanas (my brothers and sisters) who have had and continue to have the "corazon" (heart) and courage to declare their own individuality by dropping out of the gangs and stepping back from those worthless causes and so-called struggles, and who no longer contribute to the destruction of our own people.

This book is for you my brothers and sisters, so keep your head up and set your minds and hearts on things above, not on the temporary things of this world that are here today and gone tomorrow. We must all keep pressing forward for a higher education, self-respect and social status of equality, seeking a better way.

"Brethren, I do not count myself to have apprehended; but one thing I do, forgetting those things which are behind and reaching forward to those things which are ahead" (Philippians 3:13).

To my daughter, may time teach you to understand and God empower you to forgive.

And to Tia, for all your time, effort, hardwork—and for never giving up and always believing in me.

FORWARD

My original intention was to write just a two-page testimony answering the question: "If I could tell kids, teenagers and young adults something life-changing so that they would not have to go through what I have gone through in life, what would that be?" Well my brothers and sisters, the following pages are what God has put in my heart to tell you young people.

This testimony is not to gain honor and praise for myself, nor is it written to glorify my life or the gang I was in, but rather just the opposite. It is to expose the lies, deceitfulness, manipulation and brainwashing used against you young people in order to take advantage of you, use you and abuse you.

Many of my brothers who are ex-gang members have asked me why I would write this testimony knowing that it would put my life in danger. For me, this question is a very simple one to answer: at one time I was willing to spend my life behind these prison walls or die for the gang and its so-called righteous cause and struggle for the betterment of the "La Raza" (Mexican/Latino race), only to find out the "struggle" has nothing to do with "La Raza," but that it is only about destroying our Raza. The same individuals who created the gangs have destroyed their own lives and now sit in Pelican Bay Security Housing Unit (SHU), seeking whom they may devour through their lies, false sense of carnalismo (brotherly love) and intimidation. Their prey is young people whose hearts and minds they try to control through fear. I am more than willing to lay down my life to warn our young brown brothers and sisters about what is happening. I will not just turn my head aside and allow my brothers and sisters to fall victims to the Nuestra Familia (NF) and Mexican Mafia's (EME) games and allow these gangs to destroy young lives as they have destroyed their own. I cannot sit back and do nothing while watching the destruction and death of our Raza and our younger generation. "Basta!" (Enough!) is the cry of Nuestra Raza (Our Race).

So if I must die for something, I would rather die for the youth. As Emiliano Zapata said, "I would rather die standing on my own two feet, than live a lifetime on my knees!"

I will not bow down in fear and ignorance to a bunch of dope fiends doing life sentences who use people, taking advantage for their own selfish, financial gain. These are your so-called Big Homies or Carnales (members of the NF or the EME) in Pelican Bay SHU who are now expanding to the streets to spread their poison and vile.

Deep within my heart I am convinced that giving this testimony is the destiny and plan for me in life. God has allowed me to experience many different things in life, both good and bad. Through all these experiences the struggle has filled me with love, compassion and understanding for others and has given me strength and courage, making me into the man I am today in order to take on the mission and task at hand. The pen will be mightier than the sword.

So as I begin to write you, "Mi Raza," it is my earnest desire that these words will be the inspiration needed for all of you to turn from the road of self-destruction known as the "gangster's life" and "la vida loca" (the crazy life) which only leads to death or life in prison.

It is my hope and prayer that you brothers and sisters will open your hearts and minds as you read this testimony of truth and learn from my past mistakes and experiences in life, for it will save you and your loved ones a lot of heartache and grief.

"To have a fool for a son brings grief; there is no joy for the father of a fool" (Proverbs 17:21).

Someone once said, "The eyes, they are the windows of the soul." Here is some history to open your eyes and bring you out of darkness:

In 1521 conquistadors (Spanish conquerors) brought their religion to Meso-America and also introduced a new people into Mexico: children of Indian women and Spanish men as well as more than 100,000 enslaved Africans transported to Mexico beginning in the same century. That mixture of razas is the mestizo that is us, those of Mexican decent.

Every September 16th La Raza celebrates Mexico's independence. On this day in 1810 la gente (the people), led by Padre (father) Hidalgo, revolted, refusing to be governed under Spain's rule. They were tired of oppression. La Raza could no longer stand by doing nothing, allowing their women to be raped and their people to be abused and enslaved by the Gachupines (Spaniards). "Basta, Basta!" was the cry of La Raza. From north to south, people of all ages and gender filled the streets screaming, "Basta, Basta!" to the Gachupines. The time had come for La Raza to come together as one, setting aside differences between them in order to challenge and fight against the suppression of their gente.

For La Raza this was a righteous cause seeking the betterment of their pueblo. It was a struggle which would require sacrifices and the loss of life. The cause of independence was worthy of sacrifice. On August 23rd, 1821 Mexico won its independence from Spain. This struggle was truly a struggle for the betterment of Nuestra Raza. Later the U.S. and Mexican war of 1846–48 ended with the treaty of Guadalupe Hidalgo, giving the United States all of California, Utah, Colorado, Nevada and part of Wyoming.

Then the Revolution of 1910 raised the cry of injustice again. Porfiro Diaz, a dictator, who had been in power for almost thirty years was the tool of both wealthy Americanos north of the border and the rich Mexicanos from his own country. With his help wealthy landlords had driven the campesinos (peasants) off their land. El pueblo decided they could not stand this injustice any longer, allowing their rich land to be stolen from underneath their feet by the hand of foreigners and even by greedy, selfish members of their own raza. Finally Emiliano Zapata, leader from the south, and Francisco (Poncho) Villa, leader from the North, united La Raza to revolt. "Viva La Revolution!" ("Long live the revolution!")

Then later in 1962 Cesar Chavez led La Causa (The Cause), a peaceful fight for equal rights, respect, better wages, and better working conditions for the farmeros (farm workers), especially in California.

In the 1960s the Chicano Movement also began, demanding respect for Mexican culture and equality in social status. High school and college students protested, boycotting classes and taking to the streets to call for an end to institutionalized racism. College students of Mexican descent demanded programs of Chicano studies that showed respect for their race.

In 1972, groups of young Chicanos organized themselves as the Brown Berets to "serve and protect" La Raza with community programs and security. Their desire was to protect their community in non-vioent ways and give respect back to the neighborhoods where they grew up.

Now it is time for La Raza to rise up again, this time against members of our own race who are destroying our communities and taking our children captive by intimidation and violence. Our neighborhoods are infested with members of the Nuestra Familia/Norteños and the Mexican Mafia/Sureños, who are of the same heritage and background and yet, for their own selfish reasons stand contrary to our people's struggle. They take advantage of the sweat and blood of their own people's hard work and seek to destroy our young brown brothers' and sisters' lives for their own personal amusement, benefit and financial gain. They are exploiting and undervaluing our Raza's history and culture for their own self-interest. It is time to uncover their lies, reveal their evil, and refuse to be enslaved by their tyranny!

So the struggle and la causa continues today for our Raza, "Basta, Basta!" is once again the cry of el Pueblo throughout all of Aztlan! "Then you will know the truth, and the truth will set you free" (John 8:32). Can anything good come out of California's Pelican Bay State Prison Maximum Security Housing Unit?

Read and see, for the story continues…

PROLOGUE

Sadly, like so many of our youth today, I never knew my father. All I know is what my tia (aunt) Carol told me. She said, "Willie, all I know about your father is that he was an irresponsible short black man with a serious alcohol problem who abandoned your mother and you when you were still a baby." My tia was never one short for words. If you did not want to hear the truth, then you should not ask.

However she did tell me, "He really did seem to love your mother because out of your three sisters' fathers, he was the one who stayed with your mom the longest." To hear those words were music to my ears, because I had always wondered if I was conceived out of love or lust—a trick baby, if you know what I mean.

I told myself at a very young age that I would never be like my father. Sadly, I have become exactly like this stranger and in many ways far worse than him.

I was fortunate enough to have the opportunity to know my mother. I did not know her like I would have wished to, but the love she showed me is something I will forever cherish in the depths of my heart. My mother, a small heavy-set Mexican woman diagnosed with paranoid-schizophrenia,

13

suffered from a nervous breakdown. No one really knows what happened to her. My tia Carol tells me that, as a young girl, she was very smart, shy in her ways and innocent. I remember seeing a picture of her when she was young, standing with her smiling brothers and sisters, including my tia Carol. My mom had her head down, eyes closed, with her hands clasped together as if praying. All they told me was that she went out one night and returned home never to be the same. Whatever took place on that fateful night, I will never know; but from that day on she lived a life filled with loneliness, anguish, and confusion. She became a woman of the streets. She begged, borrowed, stole, and even sold her body to survive. She was a victim of abuse, both physically and mentally. Some of the abuse was self-inflicted, while most of it was inflicted by others. Many different men used her and took advantage of her. I made a promise to myself that one day I would rescue my mother and take care of her when I was old enough; however, the good Lord had different plans. I realize now He rescued her and is taking care of her.

On a gloomy October afternoon in 1985 I answered the phone quickly so my tio Pete would not wake up from his after-work nap. "Hello," I said as I picked up the phone. "Willie! Oh Mijo," she said with a deep sigh of relief, for it had been over three years since I had last seen her. Her voice was familiar yet remote, filling me with an overwhelming warmth only to be immediately replaced with a sense of fear and alarm. "Mom," I said with an anxious voice, "Where are..." was all I was able to say before I heard a gasp and stifle. "Mom," I said in a soft whisper, only to hear the sound of a click, as someone hung up the phone on the other end.

Until this day I can still visualize myself standing there in a trance-like state, dazed and confused, not wanting to comprehend what had just taken place. After a minute or so I finally gave up hope of hearing her voice and hung up the phone, knowing deep down inside something was totally wrong and I would never hear my mother's voice again.

The emptiness and deprivation I felt on that day would possess my life for the next fifteen years. Those events meant the end of the dreams and goals of a child. For me, in the moment, life no longer had any significance. Three months after that disturbing phone call I was told that my mother had passed away; that she had committed suicide. Did she really? I will never know.

That moment was the beginning of a life of rebelliousness that led to drugs, alcohol, violence, crime, prison, and gangs. For the past fifteen years, I have been on a mission of self-destruction, caught and lost in Satan's snares, trying to fill a void of emptiness inside me with all the temporary fixes of the lusts and pleasures of this world. As a result, I now sit here writing you young people from Pelican Bay State Prison SHU which houses some of California's most violent prisoners. The majority of us are or have been gang members whose conduct endangers the lives of others. We are deemed threats to the safety and security of even the general prison population. I no longer blame anyone for my actions. I realize that I chose this path to walk in life and I sit here today because of my own ignorance and foolishness.

Chapter I
THE TRUTH

The truth began to unfold for me back in 1994 in San Quentin State Prison Reception Center. Four years later after my second prison sentence and my fourth or fifth parole violation, I had acquired three 1020 confidential forms, stating that I was an active member of Nuestra Raza/Northern Structure Prison Gang, which was a second branch of the Nuestra Familia, and had been a participant in assaults and stabbings which occurred in the reception center. I was placed in "East Block" where the "hoyo" (hole) was and which also housed death row inmates. I was to be housed there while under investigation as a Nuestra Raza (NR) member. Within a month and a half, I was validated as an active NR member and given an indeterminate Security Housing Unit (SHU) sentence. This type of sentence meant that each time I came back to prison I was to do my time in the "hoyo." The Cocoran SHU or Pelican Bay SHU were the only places I could go. The fact was well known that the only way one got out of an indeterminate SHU was to "die or debrief." "Debrief" means to tell all one knows about the gang, its members, activities and functions. Well I felt I was too young to die and debriefing was the farthest thing from my mind.

A few days before Christmas at San Quentin the guards told me to trans-pack, for I would be leaving around three o' clock in the morning for Pelican Bay. I was locked up for just a parole violation so all I had to do was a little over a month, maybe close to two. Those more experienced than me had given me the rundown on what to expect, so I was at ease and looked forward to seeing and meeting all the Big Homies whom everyone talked about, all the Carnales who had started the cause and struggle of Nuestra Familia and the Norteño Movement. I knew that going to Pelican Bay Prison was really going to magnify my reputation even though I was going to be there for less than two months, that is, if I did not get into any trouble. I thought I had prepared myself physically and mentally; however, nothing I could have done would have prepared me for what I was about to experience in Pelican Bay SHU.

We arrived around 1:30 in the morning. There were four of us going to the SHU while the rest who had been transported with us were going to the mainline (general population). About four hours after arriving we were finally housed. There are two facilities that make up the SHU: C Facility which consists of twelve blocks and D Facility which has ten blocks. Each block has six sections A through F and each section has eight cells, four on the bottom and four on the top. The bottom cells are double-man cells and the top ones are single-man cells. I was housed in C-12, F section cell 222. Since it was early in the morning no one tried to get at me, out of respect for people who were sleeping. The guards uncuffed me at the pod door once it closed and cell 222 was popped open for me to go into. Already the myths were being disproved. Supposedly inmates never left their cells, and every-thing came to them; yet, here I was walking by all the other cells, up the stairs to my cell with no handcuffs. I now understood how the co-gunner working in the control booth could, whether accidently or intentionally, pop open other doors when he popped open mine. I also found out that the shower did not come to me, but was located at the end of the tier requiring me to walk all the way down the open tier. Neither was my mail read over a TV monitor nor was the yard at the back of my cell but at the back of the pod. There were many places and times when people could get to me.

The biggest surprise came in the morning when I woke up to find out that I was the only Norteño in the pod. There were two blacks downstairs, Crips from Los Angeles and one black upstairs who was a "51/50 J-Cat," as we called them. Right next to me was an older white man "lifer," a member of the Brand Aryan Brotherhood. On the other side of me was Chino, a Sureño, and downstairs in three of the four cells were four EME's and two more Sureños. It was just my luck that any other Norteños were in different pods. Even though Crips and Bloods were considered to be our allies, I never looked at them in this way for personal reasons.

All I had was my state issue bedding, clothing, state writing material, toothbrush, nasty tasting toothpowder and one bar of soap. I had no other hygiene or any reading material whatsoever. After spending a day or two later just staring at the walls and adjusting to the program, Joker from San Fernando Valley, an EME, came to my door with magazines, books and hygienes. He introduced himself, offering me, he said, "a few things to hold me over until I get my property or my home boys can send me a little care package." This encounter really messed me all up. Here in front of me was this EME member. I had always been told that the EME's were the reason why Nuestra Raza (NR) was created and why the Norteños and Sureños were at war. EME's were automatic green lights! Yet Joker went on to tell me that there was a mutual understanding among them and us in which we all stayed on a respectful level. If it happened that the doors did pop open, their people would not rush me nor did they expect me to rush them. This was the agreement among everyone in Pelican Bay SHU. I could not believe what I was hearing because I had been told that on the mainline there was straight-out war between the North and South. Those who had taught me had embedded in my mind that there is no such thing as peace, "for how can we have peace when we the 'Nuestra Familia' (NF) started this war?"

The Carnales had always reinforced this claim to me in the past. Now I was hearing about peace. Having learned weapons and warfare tactics from the Carnales, I really thought the EME's were just trying to get me comfortable and draw me near to their cells so they could spear me or shoot me with a crossbow. I found out this was not the case, for when commissary came, my neighbor Chino also hooked me up with a care package. I did not understand this part of the game. Since I was by myself with no pressure or brainwashing propaganda from the Carnales with their rules and laws, I was able to take a step back and look at things from a different perspective with an open mind. I realized then from that point on that everything was just a worthless cause full of lies and deceit. My foolish pride however would not allow me to see the truth and I continued to let the Carnales take my individuality while giving them control over my mind, body and soul, and for what? Basta mis hermanos y hermanas.

Years later I found out how the turn around came about. Secret discussions were going on between the top ranking members of the Carnales of the Mexican Mafia and the Carnales of Nuestra Familia. The mesa (table) of the NF, which consisted of five generals, put a general by the name of Black Jesse from Salinas in charge of the negotiations between the NF and the EME. The prison administration even placed these top ranking members together in the same cell block. Though Black Jesse and other Carnales worked to establish this peace treaty it became at the same time the cause of a power struggle between Carnales who were for the peace treaty and those against the peace treaty. Those Carnales who had backed the peace treaty all along quickly turned their backs on Black Jesse as if they knew nothing about it in order not to place their status in question with the majority of other Carnales of the NF who were looking to gain rank and authority. So Black Jesse became a scapegoat for those Carnales who betrayed the treaty. How quickly one's loyalty is forgotten! Black Jesse had been given a life sentence for committing murder for the NF and during the trial he was ordered by powerful Carnales to plead guilty so that another carnal could get off the hook. Yet in the blink of an eye, he was left out to dry, deemed no good by those looking out for themselves. After all these manipulations, after numerous Carnales and hermanos were deemed no good and even killed, a peace treaty exists today, though not a real peace treaty, only a cease fire established by these same Carnales.

So you ask, where is my loyalty? My loyalty is to myself and my struggle and purpose in writing this testimony to all of my brothers and sisters of different ethnicities. I direct this testimony however mainly towards Mi Raza because we are the ones out there on the streets and behind these walls looking and acting like fools, degrading our own race by killing each other while your Big Homies are sitting here in peace. "Basta!" We all need to be strong-minded individuals. Those of you who are caught up in "la vida loca" of gangs need to perceive the truth behind the lies and turn from following these blind leaders. You do not have to waste ten years of your life like I have, or even worse, end up like these blind leaders, stuck for life here in Pelican Bay SHU for an ignorant and worthless cause! These Big Homies or Carnales of the NF and EME are blind leaders of the blind and "if a blind man leads a blind man, both will fall into a pit" (Matthew 15:14).

Take a good look at where you are today and where your life is headed, following the Carnales in the so-called struggle. How many of you sit in an eight by ten cement and steel "ditch" or have been there at least once already? How many of your family members and homies have been laid to rest in a ditch at the city cemetery for wanting to imitate the Carnales and Big Homies here in Pelican Bay SHU? If some of you still think belonging to this "cause" is worth the price, let me share more with you hardheaded fools!

It is only through you, young people, that these Carnales and their gangs exist today. You so-called "gangsters, soldiers, and torpedoes" are nothing more than street corner "hookers and punks" for the Carnales. The Carnales utilize you to inculcate their ways and beliefs on your younger brown brothers and sisters and any others whom they can impose or force their beliefs on. Your younger brothers and sisters whom you school will take your place and fill your shoes after you are deemed no good, washed up or dead because of some hater or because you broke one of the childish rules or laws of the Carnales. Think about it: "A grown man being told when to get up, when to exercise and when to go to sleep by another grown man." When we were teenagers many of us did not even listen to our own parents when they told us to do something that was in our best interests. Now all of a sudden you want to follow another man's rules and orders who only wishes to destroy your life. This is the idiocy of it all!

You who act cowardly and weak-mindedly, needing another man to control you and tell you what to do, you are the ones they will use to come up and prosper off of. You are selling yourselves short, providing your services like some two dollar whore and getting nothing in return except, if you're lucky, a pat on the back, a hand shake and a lot of time behind these walls. The Carnales will persuade a lot of you young people through a false sense of carnalismo (brotherly love). Is that what you are looking for: "love and acceptance?" Instead of finding love and acceptance they will force you, by instilling fear in you, to sell and buy their drugs, commit crimes of robbery, home invasions, extortion (taxing) and even murder, all against your own Raza, your own homies, and even against your own familia and loved ones. The Carnales will order you to do such things and then have the nerve to tell you that it is a struggle for our Raza to protect our people! Basta!

These Carnales are profiting off your ignorance and sinful wickedness. They are nothing more than "dope fiend pimps" sitting here in Pelican Bay SHU and you who follow them are their prostitutes. They are worthless liars who go around winking and giving signals to deceive others. "A scoundrel and villian, who goes about with a corrupt mouth, who winks with his eye, signals with his feet, and motions with his fingers, who plots evil with deceit in his heart—he always stirs up dissension" (Proverbs 6:12-14).

So mis Hermanos y Hermanas, are my words making any sense to you yet? If not, then I suggest you pay real close attention to what I have to say next. "So peep game!"

The same Big Homies and Carnales who started all of this nonsense and continue to keep you youngsters fighting and killing each other over their cause and struggle in the streets and in all other prisons, including the California Youth Authority (CYA) have now all come to an agreement by establishing a cease fire/peace treaty with each another. There is no longer to be anymore feuding, fighting or disrespecting between anyone in Pelican Bay SHU! It no longer matters if you are Mexican Mafia, Nuestra Familia, Aryan Brotherhood, Black Guerrilla Family, a Nazi Lowrider, Sureño, Norteño, Crip, or Blood. Each and every one of these gang members here acknowledges and fully respects this treaty of peace. Yet for all you little torpedoes everywhere else and especially on the streets, this peace treaty is not to be implemented. Following such a treaty on the street would result in serious repercussions by the orders of the Big Homies! They have you youngsters living in blind fear so that you will be too scared to come to the light and think for yourselves. They tell you there is no peace. Yeah right!

In 1996 at Tracy State Prison K-Wing (The Hole) a carnal by the name of RB from Stockton established a peace treaty, saying orders had come from the carnal Big Smiley who sat on the NF Mesa and who was at that time the cause behind a major power struggle going on in D-Facility in Pelican Bay SHU. The fact was that not everyone in the Bay (Pelican Bay) was backing the treaty. For months RB was fighting a murder case for having killed a woman who was going to testify against another carnal who had committed a murder. Irregardless of his sacrifice for killing for the NF, a green light was put on RB by those in the Bay who were not supporting this peace treaty. They did not even consider his sacrifice. This man had just caught a life sentence for following orders and now he was deemed no good. He was only trying to keep in step and try to do his time in peace just like the Carnales in the Pelican Bay SHU. In this way the Carnales reward you for your services my brothers and sisters. No matter how much you do, they will never be satisfied. This story is just one of many many examples of their gratitude and appreciation for your services. Basta!

Are you young people getting the picture yet? Well if not, let me share with you a little more insight. As long as they can keep you youngsters fighting, committing crimes and killing each other on the streets, they will have the assurance that you will sooner or later end up behind these walls in the hoyos and SHU's right along side them, providing them with a young stable of fresh "meat" with naive minds to pollute and brainwash and young hearts to corrupt. If you think like a fool thinks and speak like a fool speaks, you're going to act like a fool acts and you will not even know it until you wake up one morning hemmed up behind cement walls, steel doors, and barbed wire fences, or worse, you may not wake up at all!

So at this present time and for the past nine or ten years all your Big Homies have been living together in peace and harmony, enjoying the company of their once "most hated enemies," sharing conversations, playing chess against one another over a cup of "chanate" (coffee), looking out for each other, sharing material possessions, socializing and no longer at one another's throats. They now sit within the safe confinements of their eight by ten cells, twenty-two and a half hours a day, barred from virtually all human contact. This kind of life is the life of a carnal, which you youngsters are dying and killing over to acquire. I guess you do not love your freedom or your family because you go all out, being all you can be for the "cause." In fact you must not even like women, because you are striving to be surrounded by a bunch of men for the rest of your life. Open your eyes youngsters. But wait, there is more for you young aspirants and wannabes.

Now that your Big Homies are no longer fighting or despising one another, they sit back spreading rumors and gossip behind each other's back, smiling in their own brother's face while conspiring to cross him up and take him out in order to gain rank and power, fueled by greed for their own financial benefit. You may ask about loyalty but loyalty does not really exist. The only loyalty in this game is loyalty to one's self. I was taught very early in the game: "for each his own." These people have a need to dominate and if they cannot achieve it physically, they will pursue it psychologically. They are always creating schemes to continue imposing their negative influence on you young people for one purpose: to ensure that throughout their life sentences they, the Carnales, will be supported with a steady flow of income, enabling them to live comfortably in their protective custody cells, having all the little luxuries and privileges entitled to an inmate at their disposal. They even buy expensive books to educate themselves in areas such as law, philosophy, psychology, and different languages and cultures but it is all just a front to be used as a tool to impress and brainwash you youngsters. "Of what use is money in the hand of a fool, since he has no desire to get wisdom?" (Proverbs 17:16).

You support them by putting in your loyal work and they use this support to purchase televisions, radios and numerous magazines and newspaper subscriptions to occupy their leisure time. By putting your life on the line you enable them to go to the store/canteen every month, spending the maximum amount allowed and, above all, to take care of their own family and relatives. Meanwhile they throw a few kibbles and bits to their prostitutes/soldiers every now and then to keep them happy, satisfied and obedient. These Carnales have this warped notion that they are deserving of this treatment, to be honored, praised, and supported because of who they think they are and where they are at. They boast and brag about themselves, talking about what they have done and what they can do or would do "if they were out!" Many of them are not even in touch with reality. They are living either in the past or some fantasy future. Consider the carnal "Tex" who is currently serving a life sentence. He was recently indicted by the FBI and now is wanted dead by the Carnales. His power and control are gone but his greed keeps him going. He has written an autobiography of his wasted life in prison and his involvement in Nuestra Familia. His plans are to sell this book to Hollywood and make a movie of his life, with Sylvester Stallone in the star role playing none other than "Tex" himself!

This man is one of the guys you follow and take orders from my brothers! They all have the same mentality. If they are not housed by themselves in protective custody cells designed especially for them here in Pelican Bay SHU, they tend to act like animals. If someone frightens them they become frenzied and want to kill. They devour each other as animals in a zoo would devour each other if given the chance. Everything they say and do is all just a facade to cover their greed. They continue to build their reputation and financial income at the expense of my young brown brothers' lives, those of you who keep on doing their bidding and refuse to open your eyes to see the truth. "Folly delights a man who lacks judgment, but a man of understanding keeps a straight course" (Proverbs 15:21).

All of you young people are allowing yourselves to be victimized, used as expendable pawns to be sacrificed in the Carnales' game of chess, being played on a grand, life-size scale. It is a game created by them and strictly for them, with their own set of rules and laws to be made and changed in their own best interest. As the prison game goes on, only a chosen few of these Carnales will prosper and be the victorious ones, all because they have nothing to lose and all to gain while you youngsters proceed to be their sacrificial victims. Operating on fear that fuels their hate machines, their actions represent nothing more than bigotry and prejudice against their own Raza. It is the Carnales here in Pelican Bay SHU that are winning and you, my young brothers and sisters, are the ones losing. "Basta, mi Raza!"

"The thief comes only to steal and kill and destroy…" (John 10:10).

Enough lives have been stolen, lost and destroyed and enough blood has been spilled by the hand of the Carnales and their gangs. How much longer are you young people going to play the fool for these Carnales? You are stumbling along like a bunch of dumb sheep to the slaughter, due to your lack of courage, knowledge and education. It is time to break the chains of bondage that keep you oppressed and on that road to self-destruction and death.

I write to you young men and women, exposing these Carnales in Pelican Bay SHU for what they really represent and revealing the motives behind their mountain of lies! It is time to stop being another man's pawn, playing toy and ho. It is time to grow up and be responsible, mature adults. Your loyalty is to God, your family, loved ones, your children and yourself, not to another man who just wants to use you. I have always been schooled to use others to do the dirty work, rather than getting my hands dirty. "They are like your little B!*#h, always willing to please you," said a Carnal once. Yes, he was talking about you Norteños y Sureños putting in all this work for their cause.

"Sombra (shadow)," he told me, "you can get them to do things for you by showing them a little love and affection or by instilling fear in them or you can get them to do it by manipulation, making them believe that what they are doing is for a greater purpose. It all depends on their particular weakness, since they are all weak or they would never have joined the gang, ¿qué no?" Steve, a Carnal from Stockton, said, "The easiest ones to work are the ones who think they are big and bad, always ready to do dumb stuff and get into trouble. They want everyone to know them and they want to impress you and prove to you that they are down. These are the ones we are looking for. These are the easy ones to brainwash and manipulate because they don't think for themselves."

I am more than willing to lay down my life for you brothers and sisters who are being led astray by their deception. It angers me to see the destruction of La Raza brought on by these Carnales and their stable of young two-dollar hooker/gang bangers. They used me like they are using you youngsters today, to further their cause, which I did for ten long wasted years.

Regardless of what some may think, I have found my calling and purpose in life. A true righteous cause and struggle for the betterment of mi gente. I truly believed at first that I knew what "Nuestra Raza" was all about, but now I will not sit back and turn my head and allow these "brood of vipers" to continue to lead you youngsters down that same road of darkness which I have already traveled.

So I invite you my brothers and sisters to learn from my mistakes, as I take you down the road which I have traveled in my life, the good times and bad times, literally the testimony of a Black sheep!

"Greater love has no one than this, that he lay down his life for his friends" (John 15:13).

Chapter 2
MI NEGRITO

1022 Parkway Road, "the East Side," Salinas, California.

The memories all come rushing back. How I wish I could go back and relive the young innocent years of my life! The first six years of my life, I was raised by my "nana," my mom's mother. My grandfather was killed by a drunk driver when my mom was still a young girl. I remember my nana's small, two bedroom house, always packed with her grandchildren. Luckily for Nana there was a very big backyard, with many trees. On the other side of the backyard fence was a big field. It was a child's paradise and heaven-sent because without so much space outside I do not think Nana would have been able to hang with so many kids. We all would have ended up driving her crazy.

When kids got out of hand and on Nana's nerves, all you would hear was "Patricia," with a Spanish pronunciation, "Get those kids!" Patricia, one of my tia Nuchie's children, was the oldest of all the cousins so she was Nana's enforcer. Nana would yell in Spanish and kids would fly toward the front and back doors. Whoever made it outside first was safe, but whoever got caught, got in trouble for everyone. Patricia's younger brother Timothy was the one whom I looked up to and tried to imitate in every way. Their other sister was Anna. My sisters, who also lived in Nana's house, were Denise, the oldest, then Cynthia and Brenda. I was the youngest and the only black looking kid in all the family. Since I am half Mexican and half black, I had a dark brown complexion, with black features and an afro. Nana used to call me, "Mi Negrito," (my little black boy). If seven grandchildren were not enough, Tio Louie, my mom's eldest brother, Nana's oldest son, stayed in the back house connected to a garage with his wife, Tia Hope, and their four sons. Their oldest son Louie, whom we called Luwigi, was two years older than me and my favorite play cousin. With his younger brothers Anthony, Gilbert and Joseph there was never a dull moment at Nana's house.

My mom would come and go often. As far as I knew she lived in Los Angeles. Since I was her baby and only son, she took me with her to Los Angeles on many different occasions. We always seemed to stay in different motels, never in a permanent residence. Because I was young I do not remember much about those times. One thing I do remember is that whenever my mom would come on a school day, I would always pretend to be sick just so I could stay home to be with Mom. Once I learned however that playing sick might cost me my life. One evening my mom happened to show up at Nana's house late at night. Her arrival excited me and my sister as usual. When Nana started to yell for Patricia to settle us down, we ran for cover under the blankets in our beds. A good spanking always seemed to bring on a good night sleep.

The next morning though I woke up with excruciating pain, but no one seemed to be convinced that morning. Everyone just brushed me off as if I were playing another one of my games to stay home with Mom, but it was not the case that morning. Luckily my mom knew the difference between playing and the real thing. She wanted my tia Hope to take me to the hospital, but Tia Hope was not going for it. Even my tia Carol who came by each morning refused to take me. It appeared to them that I was just faking, and they were not going be late for work on the account of me.

Mom knew something was wrong so she walked me to the city bus stop. (Well in 1975, Salinas was still considered a town, so I guess it was the town bus stop.) When we finally reached Memorial hospital I could barely walk, bent over in pain. As soon as the nurse checked me, I was immediately taken into the operating room, diagnosed with appendicitis. I stayed in the hospital for several days. Having learned my lesson about crying "wolf," I gave up playing sick and had to think of a new strategy to stay home when Mom came around.

I was in kindergarten at Fremont School. Just a few months after my appendicitis, I was in class on a day when we were painting. Instead of painting on my paper I took my paints to the back of the classroom where there was a coatroom for our jackets and started painting the walls. I painted a little and peeked my head out from behind the door looking directly at the teacher. I did not want to make too much of a mess but just enough to be sent home. It seems however that when you really want to get caught no one notices. After about four or five peeks and no reaction, I had to resort to making noise just to get the teacher's attention. When she finally did notice me, I had really overdone the paint job and braced myself for my teacher's wrath. As she pushed open the door and saw what I had done, she immediately started yelling at me. I had not only painted the wall but the balls and bikes as well that were stored there. They called my tia Carol who happened to be working as a teacher's aid in the next classroom. When she saw what I had done, she could not believe it. She was surprised not so much by my masterpiece, but by the extremes I went through just to be home with Mom. It was the first time I was suspended, and of course this was just kindergarten. Well I got my wish: the principle called Nana and she sent Mom to pick me up. Fremont School was only a couple of blocks away from my Nana's house, on the other side of El Sausal Junior High School.

At first I was so happy as my mom and I were walking home. Then I noticed Mom was not so happy. Usually she would be laughing and smiling.

Now she did not even look at me and just kept on walking, holding my hand. I could feel the disappointment and hurt coming from her. No words even had to be spoken. I knew I had messed up badly. Then I became afraid that my mom would leave when I was not around and I would miss my opportunity to go with her back to Los Angeles. I wanted to be around her as much as possible. Never before had I seen my mom so upset with me. In fact this is the only time I remember.

My mom was always happy and outgoing. She would go off sometimes on others but she never yelled at me or my sisters. In fact she had a good sense of humor. She also had a bad stuttering problem. I remember how my older cousins used to try to convince her to say the child nursery rhymes that were tongue twisters, like "Peter Piper picked a peck of pickled peppers." She could never get past saying "Peter Pi-Pi-Pie," before she would start stammering to get it out. All of us would bust up laughing and she would still try to say it right. The only reason she was able to say "Peter" was that she was familiar with that name since it was the name of my tia Carol's husband and their oldest son. I think my mom used to go along with us in these games to make us all laugh. With these good times there were also some bad times.

My tia Hope had started selling Avon jewelry and brought it over to my nana's house, leaving it overnight so Nana could look at it. With Mom at the house Nana knew she had to hide it or it would all come up missing. Nana knew the jewelry would not be safe in her room because it would be the first place Mom would ransack. So Nana hid the pink jewelry box in our room in the closet on the top shelf. I remember like it was yesterday. I woke up some time in the night to all kinds of commotion going on in my room. When I opened my eyes all I could see was my cousin Peter who had spent the night, Timothy, Patricia, my sister Denise and my mom. They were all up in our closet reaching into Tia Hope's Avon box. All their backs were turned towards me. I just closed my eyes and went back to sleep.

The next day after everyone got off work and out of school, my tia Hope was steaming mad along with my tia Carol. Everyone was gathered in the kitchen and accusations were flying everywhere at everyone. All the older kids were questioned because the jewlery box was too high in the closet for us little kids to reach. Everyone denied any involvement so the accusations came back to Mom who was always the number one suspect. My tia Carol said, "Lollie," (my mom's name was Dolores but everyone called her Tia Lollie or just Lollie) "just return the jewelry." Well Mom was not going to return anything and even if she wanted to do it she could not return the jewelry because she did not have it all. Rather than giving up everybody involved in the heist, she just stormed out of the house, cussing and cursing. When Mom got upset she had a mouth on her and she was hot that day. As everyone continued to argue, I followed Mom out the front door. She did not even acknowledge me and headed down the sidewalk without looking back. I stood there and just watched her go until she turned the corner. I did not see her any more. I could have said something but I just kept my mouth shut and let my mom take all the blame.

Not long afterwards our lives as kids would suddenly be turned upside down. One morning as we were going out the door to school, Tia Carol was there with Nana sitting in a chair at the door as each of us headed out the door. Tia Carol told us to give Nana a hug and a kiss. When my turn came I gave Nana a big hug and kiss on the cheek. "Oh mi Negrito!" Nana said with sadness in her voice. Later when we came home from school we found out that Nana was in the hospital for the terminally ill. She had been sick for some time and refused to be operated on. She stayed with us kids until she could no longer bear the internal pain. She passed away a short time later. I did not even realize Nana was sick for she showed no symptoms.

Nana was a strong woman and did not have the habit of showing weakness. Once my cousin Timothy came home from El Sausal Junior High after getting into a fight or riot which was something of a habit for him. His arms

33

and face had all kinds of slashes as if he had been whipped with something. As always he tried to hide what happened from Nana and snuck into the room where we happened to be changing our school clothes. Nana must have sensed something was wrong because she came in a couple of minutes later with her thick black belt in her hand. As soon as she saw Tim, she started swinging, reminding him in Spanish how many times she had told him about fighting. Tim, trying not to get hit, grabbed my sister Brenda but that did not stop Nana. By the time she finished, the whole room of kids was crying.

One day, when I was in my early twenties, I asked my tia Carol to tell me what Nana had died from. "Lung cancer," she said. "Lung cancer!" I said in surprise. "I don't remember her smoking!" "That's because she never smoked in front of you guys," she said. As I look back I am amazed at how much the times and people have changed since 1976. Today parents not only smoke cigarettes, but weed, crack and crank in the presence of their children. Some even go as far as purposefully exposing their children to gangs and violence, thinking it is so cute to dress a two-year-old child in gang banging colors and teach them to throw up gang signs. These are parents who have no shame or regret whatsoever. We continue to pass this destructive behavior from one generation to another. When will we wise up and begin to think about the consequences of our actions and the impact of our destructive example as parents or even as older brothers, sisters, uncles, aunts and cousins? This destructive lifestyle must end with us here and now.

We must ask ourselves what example are we setting for our younger loved ones who look up to us for guidance. We need to ask ourselves the "would" questions? Would we want our kids to be drug addicts? Would we want our kids to be caught up in gangs? Would we want our kids to be in prison for life? Would we want our children to end up dead because of the examples we have set for them to follow?

I once had a friend who had just been released from jail and her son had just run from the youth center for delinquent kids. For a half an hour she was all in her son's ear, telling him what she did not want him to do and with whom she did not want him hanging around. Then, just ten minutes later, she was on the phone talking about drugs and a gun to the same people she was telling her son not to hang around with, right in front of him! I have to admit I have done the same things.

It is time my young brown brothers and sisters to leave our old foolish, destructive attitudes in the past and have the will and determination to adopt new, more meaningful and fulfilling dreams. We have to have the willingness to stand out from the crowd of blind fools and weak followers. You youngsters must have the desire to strive for a better education, respect, and social status of equality. I am not talking about the kind of respect that the gang teaches which is pure hatred for your own kind. I am talking about setting an example of righteousness, treating your fellow brown brothers and sisters with dignity and respect just as you would like to be treated. Then you and your loved ones will be able to live in peace and harmony, just like your so-called Big Homies and Carnales here in Pelican Bay (SHU). You must not allow a street name, or town, or number, or the color of a rag to deceive you. You must not allow greed for power, drugs, and wealth to be the reason for selling yourselves short in life and setting the same destructive example for your young family members and loved ones to follow. "Basta mi Raza!"

"Dear children, do not let anyone lead you astray. He who does what is right is righteous, just as he is righteous. He who does what is sinful is of the devil, because the devil has been sinning from the beginning" (1 John 3:7–8).

Chapter 3
NORTH SIDE

My nana's greatest concern was the future welfare of her grandchildren. She had stipulated before her death that whoever took in the kids would also get the house. Tia Carol and Tio Pete who already had two sons of their own committed themselves to adopting my sisters, Cynthia and Brenda, and me. My oldest sister Denise had run away right after Nana's funeral. She followed my mom only to get caught up in the streets of Los Angeles. Tia Carol and Tio Pete also took in my cousin Patricia and her brother Timothy. So once again we had more than a full house.

I think out of all my nana's grandchildren, Timothy took her death the hardest. After her death he did not care about anything or anyone. All I remember is that he was always coming home bloody, with bruises or black eyes from fighting or getting into riots at El Sausal Junior High. He taught me at an early age not to be scared of anyone. "I don't care how big or how old they are, you better not back down from no one. Because no matter if they kick your butt, they are going to think twice about trying to get with your program, and they will respect you more for not backing down." To me Tim was like the big brother or the father I never had. We would fight a lot even though he was five years older than me and could toss me around like a rag doll. I would not give up and with tears running down my face, I would scream and yell trying to punch him, kick him or bite him, only to be tossed around some more.

We lived at Nana's house for over a year and then Tio Pete and Tia Carol decided to buy a bigger home to raise all of us kids. They found a four bedroom home in North Salinas. I do not know exactly what happened but when we moved from the East Side to the North Side, I went through a major change in attitude and character. No sooner had I started school than I was getting into trouble. I was fighting anyone and everyone who wanted to try me. Not only was I fighting but I also acquired a real smart mouth and became a class clown. I do not know the cause of all this disruptive behavior. These changes might have been due to the lack of attention that I used to get or the fact that I was no longer allowed to go with my mom nor was my mom coming around either.

From the third grade to the sixth grade, I must have been suspended from school close to fifty times. Why they did not just expel me I will never know. During the summer of 1983, before the seventh grade, at age thirteen, I started experimenting with drugs. At first I was just using marijuana, then acid, then alcohol, then coke and before I knew it, I was smoking PCP and found it to be my drug of choice. I loved the feeling of not being able to feel anything. School became unimportant. Finally I was kicked out of junior high school for fighting and using drugs. My tia Carol tried to enroll me in a stricter middle school, but I only lasted a week there. I will admit I was a school bully. I had known a few kids at that school and inquired about who was the baddest or at least who thought he was the baddest. That same day I got into it with a tall white kid. Before I even got home the school had contacted my tia Carol, informing her that her son was not going to work out in their school. After this incident the school district put me into independent studies, a kind of continuation school for those who could not hang in a regular school. Independent studies left me with too much time on my hands.

I was already a ward of juvenile court after stealing a bike for one piece that I could use to fix my beach cruiser. It was just my luck that the derailler that shifts the gears did not even work on the stolen bike. To top it off my home boy Emillo had dared me to steal the bike in the first place, a challenge of course that I could not refuse. That incident was the beginning of my troubles with being caught up in the juvenile court system.

It did not take long for me to get hooked on drugs. I had to have weed every day and started stealing from my tio Pete or whoever else had money in the house, with the exception of my tia Carol. For some reason, I could not steal from Tia Carol. Not only was I stealing at home, but I also became really good at stealing from stores. When I could not get money for drugs, I would hit the nearby grocery store and steal a bottle of hard liquor to satisfy myself by getting skunk drunk. When I really needed money I went out to pull burglaries. I remember the home boys Angel and Rodney telling me that some guy who lived down the street had shown them some guns. So the next day while everyone was at school and work, I headed for this guy's house and got in through the garage. Once I got inside I could not find the guns and ended up stealing jewelry, money, and anything small I could get rid of to get some dope.

I had just started high school and had played sick that day so I could break into that house. Like all impulsive people I did not think before doing things. Had I thought carefully I would not have done this burglary since the people knew me. I rode my bike or walked down this street at least four or five times a day, not only to and from school, but also to the drug spot, "Block Street," where all the older home boys hung out and sold drugs. It was easy for the people to figure out who had burglarized their house. That evening when I got home my tia Carol knew that some way or some how I had something to do with it since the police came looking for me. About a month later I was finally charged and a short time afterwards I was found guilty and ordered to serve thirty days in juvenile hall.

So on December 5th, 1984 I was taken into custody. It was my first time in juvenile hall. The hardest part was leaving my high school sweetheart for thirty days. She would eventually become my baby's mama ten years later. I must admit I was kind of scared when I was first locked up in the hall, but I settled in quickly. The fact that other kids were there whom I knew from junior high and other places and who also knew me made adjustment easy. Since the time my cousin Timothy had done weekends there, I had always had this sick desire to see the inside of juvenile hall. Well I got my wish and I would see the inside of the hall many more times after this. After about the third time, going to the hall meant nothing, for every time I saw the same familiar faces. I was in and out of juvenile hall so many times that the court finally declared me a "serious habitual offender."

That we could see the county jail from our cells made us wonder how county jail compared to juvenile hall. That the inmates could smoke in county jail and only had to do a third of their time made all of us youngsters want to go there. I remember a guest speaker coming to the hall one time who made us even more excited about spending time in "county." He was an ex-gang member of Nuestra Familia who was also a born-again Christian. The irony of his presentation was that he came to talk about what God had done in his life and could do in ours; but the only thing that stuck in my head was the power and fear he got from others, which I interpreted as respect, and how he could go into an empty cell and come out with some type of weapon he had made. After this man's visit at the hall I started asking questions about the NF. I even went back to my cell to try to make a weapon.

In January of 1986, after being out of juvenile hall for about two weeks, I was walking home with my girlfriend. As we were crossing the school yard my cousin Eric came up to us riding his bike and barking out orders that his mom wanted me home immediately. I knew that I was in trouble for something and for the rest of the way home I tried to figure out what I had done or had not done. I was always in some kind of trouble.

As I walked into the house I noticed my tia Carol in the living room along with my sister Cynthia. My sister Brenda had run away a few months earlier and was living in Santa Cruz in a group home. "Willie, I need to talk with you and Cynthia alone," my tia Carol said. So we headed to my room and closed the door. As we sat down on the bed, my tia started talking to us. "I don't know how else to tell you guys this, but I received a phone call today from a detective down in Los Angeles. He told me that your mom is dead." My sister started crying but I was just stuck in a daze, not wanting to believe it. "Willie, Willie!" my tia was saying before I snapped out of the daze. I could only think to ask how she died. "Suicide," my tia said. Upon hearing that I started reminiscing about the phone call I received a few months earlier. I knew deep inside that my mom did not commit suicide as the police believed. My tia assured me that the detectives said there was no foul play. They said my mom had jumped into a scalding hot tub of water and she died after her body went into shock from third degree burns on most of her body.

We traveled down to Corona, California to bury my mom next to my great-grandmother, Mama Chuy. I talked to my oldest sister Denise who told me that she had gone to visit my mom at the home where she lived under the supervision of caregivers, some lady and man. Denise said that my mom was very skinny and scared to talk with her in front of her caregivers. When she tried to take my mom out by herself the caregivers would not let her do it. My sister's words convinced me even more that we did not know the whole story about my mom's death. It seemed to me that just because she was a street person and had paranoid schizophrenia, she was a nobody and her death did not warrant an in-depth investigation. I decided to take matters into my own hands. I asked my tia Carol to call the caregiver and see if they were going to come to the funeral. They assured her they were. In my mind I was going to show them how it feels to lose someone you love dearly. I had a bad habit of always carrying knives with me. Though I had never used them on anyone, there is a first time for everything. I wanted them to feel my hurt, my pain and my anger. After telling our family they would be there, they did not even have the decency to show up and pay their respects at the memorial or burial. The fact that they did not come created more anger inside me. The funeral was going to be a closed casket memorial; however, my sister Denise and Brenda wanted to see Mom and so did I. We were the only ones who approached the casket to see her. I do not remember my sisters leaving my side, but I must have been there looking at my mom by myself for some time because my tio Bobby finally came up behind me and whispered that that was "enough mijo," gently turning me away. As I turned, I searched the church pews for the unfamiliar faces of the caregivers but to no avail.

A few days after the funeral we came back to Salinas and, filled with anger and pain, I went off the hook. After returning to school for a couple of weeks, I was kicked out of North Salinas High. A short time later I ran away from home. My home boy's tia had her own place behind a liquor store and so I moved in with her. All I had to do was keep her and me high and drunk every day. The place became a neighborhood hangout. I was getting social security checks every month for $250 and I also started selling marijuana on Block Street, hanging out with the older home boys. I had become so skilled at fighting that kids my age were no match and I was fighting guys in their early and mid twenties. As a young teenager loaded with hurt, pain, and anger, I blamed everyone and anyone for the death of my mother and for the hand I was dealt in life. I got caught up in "la vida loca" of the streets, looking up to the Big Homies. I was blind with ignorance and very naive to believe that partying, getting high, having sex, committing crimes, selling dope and especially beating others up, were all ways to rid myself of my hurt and pain and to release all my anger. In a way life seemed effortless, filled with excitement and so self-satisfying that it seemed to fill the emptiness inside me. As long as I kept myself occupied with all that the streets had to offer, a pocket full of dope, hanging out with the homies, and having fun with the girls, there was nothing to worry about. It was only when the party was over and my pockets were empty that all the hurt and pain came flooding back, leaving me to feel more hollow than before.

Nevertheless I had acquired a reputation for being down for anything and capable of handling my business. I lived for the attention and respect I got from the girls and the homies, young and old. Amazingly though when I was finally thrown back into juvenile hall for stealing a bottle of tequila and a carton of cigarettes, for some odd reason I welcomed the time off the streets, maybe because the pain and hurt were becoming unbearable. The guards gave me a phone call and so I called my tia Carol. As soon as I heard her voice I began to cry.

I am so grateful that the Lord placed my tia Carol in my life because no matter how much heartache and grief I caused her, she never gave up on me. The more I got myself into trouble, the more love she showed me and the harder she worked to teach me right from wrong, and to instill good values in me. At the time I was not listening to her daily lectures. "Willie, I know you don't want to hear it, but you're gonna hear it anyways, because maybe it will sink in," she would say. Many times she brought tears to my eyes.

Now that I am older and wiser, I have to thank God for her and all her time and effort she unconditionally spent trying to raise me right. No matter what happens in our life there will always be a special someone in our life, whether that person is a grandmother, an aunt or cousin, a sister, or even a teacher or pastor, to help us through life's difficulties. We may refuse the instructions and teachings of those whom God places in our lives to help guide us down that smooth and righteous path, but they are there for us because He puts them there. We choose by our own free will to go in the opposite direction and do things our own way, leading only to a life of confusion and destruction.

At that moment in my life "la vida loca," the role of a so-called gangster, was the only realistic "career objective" I could imagine for myself. In my eyes this goal was more realistic than hoping to become someone like my tia was always talking about. She would say, "Willie, you're a smart kid and you can be someone in life. I see how all the neighborhood kids look up to you. You could be a counselor, a doctor, a lawyer, or whatever you want to be in life. Your mom always used to say that you were going to be somebody in life." At such moments the tears would come gushing out because I knew I had already made a mess of my life at such a young age. I was a drug addict, an alcoholic, a thief, a liar and a drug dealer. I was a very confused youngster and I was destroying my life.

"Though my father and mother forsake me, the Lord will receive me" (Psalm 27:10).

Chapter 4
CALLED

I was busted for that tequila and carton of cigarettes on a Saturday. On Sundays there was always a church service in juvenile hall. The only reason a lot of us went to the service was to get out of our cells. That Sunday there was no special guest, just an old lady from the Salvation Army who came every Sunday. The message she gave us was simple, telling us how God could change our lives and take away our hurt and pain that many of us feel inside that lead us to live a destructive life. Everything she was saying hit home hard. I began feeling this ache in my heart as if something was missing, a yearning, a need. At the end of her message she asked if we wanted to accept Jesus Christ into our hearts. Of course our pride would not let us respond to her words; we could not show weakness.

After church was over I stayed back. When everyone had returned to their cells I asked the Salvation Army lady to pray for me. She asked me if I wanted Jesus in my life and if I believed that He died for my sins and rose from the dead. I told her I believed because I was not blind nor was I ignorant of God and His Son Jesus Christ. My tia Carol had taken me and my sisters to catechism before we moved to North Salinas.

She asked me to repeat a prayer and no sooner had I begun, than tears of pain and hurt came gushing out. I felt as if I had no control over what was happening to me. The weird part about this experience was that I felt a peace inside me that was unexplainable. The pain, hurt and anger seemed to be flowing out of me through my many tears. I did not want the moment to end. But when I was done repeating the "sinner's prayer" as it is called, my pride got the best of me. I quickly wiped away my tears so none of the other youngsters would notice that I had been crying.

Back in my cell, I quickly picked up my Bible and started reading, hoping to get that feeling of peace again, but nothing happened. The woman had told me to keep reading the Bible and praying. I did what she told me to do and a week later I was back on the streets and back home with my tia Carol and family. I told myself, "No more drugs!" But I was surrounded by the life I knew I needed to escape.

There were a lot of home boys of mine who all hung out together so we started a little click and called ourselves the "North Side Locos." From our front yard we could see the back school fence where we used to hang out and get high and drunk. I had just gotten out of juvenile hall when I saw a couple of homies getting high so I went over there on my bike. When I came up to them they offered me some weed as always, knowing that I was a big ol' stoner like them. When I refused and told them I had stopped because I was going to church, they all laughed at me. I told them I did not need it. "Yeah, right!" said French Bro, who was half black and half French. "I'll bet you by next week you'll be smoking weed!"

He was right. The next day I started smoking weed again. I do not know what I was thinking. I thought I could hang out and overcome the temptation to smoke or drink. I found out that I could not hang out without doing the drugs too. A friend of the family helped me buy a car and once again I ran away to live with my high school sweetheart and her family. Her parents were very lenient to the point that I pretty much did what I wanted. I started hanging out at the end of town called Santa Rita "aka" Bahamas as we called it. This neighborhood was the new drug spot and cocaine was the preferred drug.

When I first started hanging out I only snorted cocaine while everyone else was smoking crack cocaine. I used to get my clown on by telling the homies they were crack head "smokers." I used to suck my cheeks in so my face looked all sucked up. People say though that the same thing that will make you laugh, will make you cry. Later when I took my first hit from a crack pipe, I was sprung like a research monkey on crack. My habit became so bad that I moved out of my girlfriend's house and starting living on the streets, hustling everybody in order to get high. At first I was robbing and stealing to come up. Then I quickly realized that I could just sell dope, cocaine and rock, and with the profit I could be getting high for free plus have money in my pocket to do as I pleased.

It was not long before I ran into my home boy's aunt, with whom I had stayed when I first ran away. Nini was her name. She had an apartment right on the other side of the mall and she smoked rocks. Soon I moved in with her. As long as we continued to smoke, everything was good. I got so bad, that I was smoking more rocks than I was selling. At the same time I had to take care of Nini, a home boy named David and his ol' lady Lisa. After a month or so all that mattered was just hustling to get high. I owed all my connections. The only reason they continued to mess with me was because of all the business I brought them and the fact I was easy to get along with. I knew how to manipulate people and took advantage of every situation for my own benefit and interest. Nini had come right in time. I had been staying at this white guy's house who sold weed. We had hooked him on smoking rocks in Santa Rita. Because of all the traffic and crack heads in and out of his place, he was evicted. I needed a place to stay and along came Nini, so we hooked up again. But then in February of 1989, the cops would rain on my party.

It was a Friday night and I had just picked up a little something to hold me off until the connection came through. Nini and I had just taken a hit and I passed the pipe to Lisa when I heard a knock on the door. I went to the peep hole and looked out only to see a short Mexican guy around thirty-eight or forty years old. Just the day before I had asked Lisa what her dad looked like since she said that he sold coke. Well this guy at the door fit Lisa's dad's description to the tee. So I backed away and yelled at Lisa that her dad was at the door. She came out of the room and looked through the peep hole only to say that it was not her dad. By then Nini was at the door and just opened it. I jumped behind the door, looking through the crack of the door. The Mexican guy asked for "Maria" which was Nini's real name. Nini said, "Yes?" "You don't remember me," the guy said. Nini, who was all high, got an attitude and said, "Who the hell are you?!" In that moment the guy said, "Salinas Police Department!" All I heard was a rumble of feet coming up the stairs. I turned and tried to break for the patio door. As I put my hands on the latch, a big ol' white cop grabbed me from behind and slammed me on the living room floor. I turned my head up only to see the barrel of a gun. They handcuffed us all and sat me at the kitchen table to read me my rights. As I sat at the table the phone started ringing off the hook and when the woman officer answered it, she spotted a twenty dollar rock on the counter right next to the phone. I had been looking at it since they sat me down. Had they waited a half hour longer they would have busted me with a half ounce or more. The cops told everybody who called to come over; that I was tied up at the moment. They said in the police report that over thirty people called within the hour they were there and over half of them came to score dope.

My tia Carol had constantly warned me that living the lifestyle I was living would bring consequences. Despite her counsel I continued to live "la vida loca" and now it was time to face the consequences just as Proverbs 19:29 says, "Penalties are prepared for mockers and beatings for the backs of fools." I believe when I began to surrender my life to Jesus Christ a couple of years earlier in juvenile hall, God was preparing me for the trials ahead. Even though I went back to my same old ways, He says in His word, "I will never leave you nor forsake you." He called me for His plan and His purpose and allowed me to experience all that I have seen for a greater purpose of which I was not even aware at the time. This purpose is the reason why I sit here today writing to you young brothers and sisters. God is calling and has called many of us, but few are chosen. So my brothers and sisters, before I start the next chapter of my testimony, let me share a very powerful and moving story of one that was called and chosen by God to open the eyes of the blind.

According to Charles Colson in his book, *Loving God* (copyright 1996, Zondervan Publishing House), in the fourth century there lived an Asiatic monk who had spent most of his life in a remote community of prayer, raising vegetables for the cloister kitchen. When he was not tending his garden spot, he was fulfilling his vocation of study and prayer.

Then one day this monk named Telemachus felt that the Lord wanted him to go to Rome, the capital of the world – the busiest, wealthiest, biggest city in the world. Telemachus had no idea why he should go there, and he was terrified at the thought. But as he prayed, God's directive became clear.

How bewildered the little monk must have been as he set out on the long journey on foot, over dusty roads heading westward with everything he owned on his back. Why was he going? He did not know. What he would find there? He had no idea. But, obediently, he went. Telemachus arrived in Rome during the holiday festival.

The Roman rulers kept the ghettos quiet in those days by providing free bread and special entertainment called circuses. When Telemachus arrived, the city was full of excitement from the recent Roman victory over the Goths. In the midst of the jubilant commotion, the monk looked for clues as to why God had brought him. So Telemachus let the crowds guide him and the stream of humanity soon led him into the coliseum where the gladiator contests were to be staged. He could hear the cries of the animals in their cages beneath the floor of the great arena and the clamor of the contestants preparing to do battle. He knew that God must have a special purpose for him.

The gladiators marched into the arena, saluted the emperor and shouted, "We who are about to die salute thee!" Telemachus shuddered. He had never heard of gladiator games before but had a premonition of awful violence.

The crowd had come to cheer men, who for no reason other than amusement, would murder each other. Human lives were offered for entertainment. (Just as your lives are offered for the entertainment of the Carnales, the Big Homies in Pelican Bay SHU).

When the monk understood what was going to happen, he realized he could not sit still and watch such savagery. Neither could he leave and forget. He jumped to the top of the perimeter wall and cried, "In the name of Christ, forbear!"

The fighting began of course. No one paid the slightest heed to the puny voice. So Telemachus pattered down the stone steps and leapt onto the sandy floor of the arena. He made a comic figure – a scrawny man in a monk's habit dashing back and forth between muscular, armed athletes. One gladiator sent him sprawling with a blow from his shield, directing him back to his seat. It was a rough gesture, though almost a kind one. The crowd roared.

But Telemachus refused to stop. He rushed into the way of those trying to fight, shouting again, "In the name of Christ, forbear!" The crowd began to laugh and cheer him on, perhaps thinking that he was part of the entertainment.

Then his movement blocked the vision of one of the contestants. The gladiator saw a blow coming just in time. Furious now, the crowd began to cry for the interloper's blood.

"Run him through," they screamed. The gladiator he had blocked raised his sword and with a flash of steel struck Telemachus, slashing him down across his chest and into his stomach. The monk gasped once more, "In the name of Christ, forbear!"

There were other forces at work, of course, but that innocent figure lying in the pool of blood crystallized the opposition, and one by one from the greatest to the least, people started standing up and leaving. That contest was the last of the gladiatorial contests in the Roman Coliseum. Never again did men kill each other for the crowd's entertainment in the Roman arena.

Think about it my young brothers and sisters. How many lives will have to be sacrificed in our streets before we can bring a halt to decades of senseless killing and young men dying for another man's entertainment? "Basta mi Raza, Basta!"

"And we know that in all things God works for the good of those who love him, who have been called according to his purpose. For those God foreknew he also predestined to be conformed to the likeness of his Son, that he might be the first born among many brothers. And those he predestined, he also called; those he called, he also justified; those he justified, he also glorified. What, then, shall we say in reponse to this? If God is for us, who can be against us?" (Romans 8:28-31)

God knows the future better than we know the past and present.

Chapter 5
MCJ

I was booked and charged in the Monterey County Jail (MCJ) with possession of a controlled substance and given a $10,000 bail. The guards housed me in a section called E-pod. The only person I knew was a guy named Donald who had attended Mt. Toro School with me so I just kicked it with him. He introduced me to the other Big Homies who looked at me kind of funny because I looked black but I did not let their stares bother me. I slept downstairs with the Raza and ate at the same table as the Raza. I would not even acknowledge or talk to the Blacks who also looked at me funny. About four days later, while we were eating dinner, a shot caller for the Blacks finally hit me up. He must have been calling me for a while because by the time I realized he was calling me the whole pod was looking at me. I asked him what was up and, with a slight attitude in his voice, he asked me if I was a brother. I was a little lighter than him, with a bigger afro than he had and I told him straight up, "No, I ain't no brother," and kept on eating. There were a couple of giggles at the table as well as some dirty looks from the Blacks, but I was not tripping.

About a week later a black guy named Lawrence, whom I knew really well, came in. When I started hanging out with him, it did not take long for him and the other blacks to try to manipulate me. They told me that being half Mexican did not matter. Since I looked black, if I ever went to prison, the Mexicans would not back me up. After hearing their tales I started hanging out with the blacks and even moved upstairs with them. Luckily before they could really brainwash me I was OR (released on my own recognizance) with the promise to return for sentencing. I was out for thirty days and moved in with my girlfriend Lisa and her mom.

Lisa however set me up for one of my home boys named Troubles because I had disrespected his girlfriend. Right after she received a phone call she walked out of the apartment to go wash clothes. As soon as she walked out the door, my home boy, his brother who just had gotten out of prison and who was a member of the prison gang known as the Northern Structure (which I knew nothing about at the time) and another home boy came walking in. When Troubles immediately rushed me, I could smell the alcohol on his breath and knew that if I started putting hands on him the other two would not hesitate to jump in. So I let him wrestle with me. About the time that we got close to the front door, Troubles told them to get a knife. When his brother went for the knife in the kitchen, that was my cue. I threw Troubles off me and gave him a few punches to the face, breaking for the door. I had the door open and stuck my head through when the other home boy kicked the door and caught me in the head. I stumbled outside, escaping the stabbing and ass whipping. The next day I went to court and was sentenced to three years felony probation and six months in jail. I was back in custody.

I was housed in C-Wing for a couple of days and then moved to the Mainline at MCJ. While I was there I found out the truth about kicking it with the Raza. Apparently a lot of the older home boys went to school with my older cousin Patricia and my sister Denise. Furthermore Lisa's cousin Pit Bull was also in there with me. "Hey check this out, homie, now that we know where you come from and your gente you're one of us," said my home boy Bobby. I explained to them what the blacks had told me and why I had jumped ship back in E-pod. "Don't listen to them homies, you're Raza. No matter how you look, in your heart you're Raza." There was another homie in there named Mark who was also half Mexican and half Black; so he and I became Road Dogs.

A few weeks later Bobby hit up Mark and me. He wanted us to assist him in breaking into a black guy's locker who had burned his brother for some drugs . It just so happened that a couple of days earlier I had gotten into an argument with this same black guy, so I was still holding a grudge and readily agreed along with Mark. We made plans to do the hit at dinner chow. Right before the yard closed, I brought a horseshoe in to break the lock. When everybody left to go to dinner, Bobby broke the lock and took off while Mark and I emptied out the locker. We put all of this dude's stuff in another locker, including about $250.00 worth of commissary and about $100.00 cash.

After we were done I told Mark not to go to chow but he did not listen. He was the last one in line behind the blacks who were last in line, including this guy whom we had just robbed. Instead of going to chow I went to the TV room and waited for people to come out from the chow hall. Then I went to the yard for awhile. When I finally decided to come back into the wing, the deputies were already around this guy's locker. I was on the other side of the wall and leaned over as if I did not know what happened. In front of the deputies and blacks I said, "Damn, that's messed up!" They knew though that Mark had something to do with the broken locker because he had been last in line. The Blacks threatened to beat up Mark and me until we told them who did it. The next day they tried to jump Mark on the yard. Luckily I saw two blacks running and just happened to get up to see where they were running to. I saw they had Mark up against the fence. I yelled to the home boys that they were jumping Mark and took off running. At full speed I leaped into the air and threw an elbow to the side of the head of the guy whose locker we had just robbed and dropped him. All the homies came rushing behind me. Before a complete riot could begin, the deputies came running and everyone backed off. That night tensions were high but nothing kicked off.

The drama continued though the next morning when some big Samoan named Wack, who hung around with the blacks we had robbed, started some funk with me. When I asked him what he was looking at, he hit me over the head with a pair of shoes he had in his hand like I was a little "poo-butt." We exchanged a few words and headed out to the yard to handle it, though to be quite honest my heart was beating fast and hard out of fear. All the home boys were asleep and the blacks were following right behind us running their mouths. I do not know how it happened, but once on the yard we squared off and he threw a punch that came at me in slow motion. I took full advantage of the swing and before anyone knew it he was on the ground talking about "Awright! Awright!" I felt really good with the attention this fight brought me but I was deceiving myself and setting myself up to be used.

Of course he ended up telling on me and I was put in C-Wing for ten days. When I went to roll up my property, Mark was laying in bed with bumps on his face and a fat lip. The deputy saw him and told him to roll up too. So we both spent ten days in C-Wing. While we were there the homies did not send us anything from what we had stolen. When we got back everything we had taken from the locker was gone and we just got a bunch of negativity in return. Bobby was saying that he called the shot and ordered us to do the job. The homies were mad because they all backed up Mark and me when Mark was getting jumped, yet Bobby did not help. So everyone decided that Bobby had to go and that Mark and I would remove him.

At first the homies were saying that we should put some locks in a sock, but I told them I did not need that. I was no coward and I had already proven what I could do. After lights went out Mark and I went to Bobby's bed and gave him a rude awakening with a fury of blows to his head and body, leaving him there all beat up. I loved all the attention and respect I was getting for being down. After this incident the so-called Big Homies really started using me and taking advantage of my willingness to be accepted by them. The homies gave me the job of rolling up all those whom they did not want in our wing. After a week of doing this work the deputies rolled me up and put me in lock down for the rest of my time. While the Big Homies enjoyed the benefits and privileges of the Mainline because of all I had done for them, I got nothing in return.

Because I was young, stupid and willing, I became easy prey for the Carnales and the Big Homies of Nuestra Familia, a prison gang created by a bunch of dope fiends who were drop-outs from the EME. They were trying to take over the drug empire established behind the walls of California's Department of Corrections (CDC) by other dope fiends, from the very same EME.

"It is not good to have zeal without knowledge, nor to be hasty and miss the way" (Proverbs 19:2). This statement describes me. I had lots of zeal, lots of energetic enthusiasm; but I had no knowledge, no understanding of what was really happening. Everything that I was willing to steal was handed over to the Big Homies to help buy their own dope to get high. Everyone I was ordered to roll up was someone they owed, or disliked or someone who was snitching on them. "Welcome to the cause and struggle of Nuestra Familia and the Norteño Movement" which, at the time, I knew nothing about.

When I was released from jail, I moved in with my cousin Patricia. Her husband must have heard about my activities in jail because he started making comments about me being a soldier in jail. Honestly I did not understand what he was talking about. I wish I had understood at that time and realized the wreck I was headed for, but I was young and naive.

Now I sit here on the other side of the fence, an ex-gang member or dropout (DO), a name on the gang's no good "hit list," "in the hat" as these convicts call it, "with a green light on my life." Simply put, I am to be dealt with, assaulted, sliced, stabbed, killed, or whatever the opportunity presents.

Now I am no longer blind. After so many years my eyes are opened to the truth behind the Carnales' lies and propaganda that they used to control me and that now controls so many young people who are caught up in "la vida loca." You young men and women of tomorrow who are fighting and killing one another, you are destroying your lives and the lives of others all for the benefit and personal financial gain of individuals serving life sentences. These dope fiends whom you revere so much are selfish, overly-sensitive and easily hurt, envious, jealous, and arrogant. They have dedicated what is left of their lives to the destruction of their own race by taking advantage of you young people and your ignorance in order to achieve their own ends. They use fear, dishonesty, and manipulation to mislead you young brown people, poisoning your hearts and minds. Basta, mi Raza! Basta!

"Not a word from their mouth can be trusted; their heart is filled with destruction" (Psalm 5:9). *"I tell you, my friends, do not be afraid of those who kill the body and after that can do no more. But I will show you whom you should fear; Fear him who, after killing of the body, has power to throw you into hell"* (Luke 12:4-5).

You will serve whomever you fear. If you fear man (the Carnales), you will serve them. If you fear God, you will serve him. I know that I would rather serve God than man who is absolutely nothing before God!

Chapter 6
CDC 1990

When I was released from jail in the summer of 1989, a month before my nineteenth birthday, I started claiming to be a Norteño and Norte. (a Northern Mexican from Northern California). I did not even know the history behind this gang. All I knew was that I wanted to be a part of it because all the homies were all about it and they accepted and embraced me, showing me some carnalismo (brotherly love). If I had been as smart as I wanted people to think I was, I would have realized that all the words were false, that there was no love, honor or loyalty among the Norteños and especially among the Nuestra Familia (NF).

I do not know how but I lasted out on the streets for about eight months. I was heavily into drugs and deep into smoking PCP. I was so deep and smoking so much that one day while I was at my sister's house I went out on the patio to smoke a double liner, which had double the amount of PCP that a regular lenyo (joint) had. After that, all I remembered was waking up at Natividad Hospital. I had overdosed. I do not know how long I had been out, but when I woke up I was strapped down to a bed surrounded by five or six police officers. As my eyes adjusted to the light, the cops began reading me my rights and the nurse took my blood. Still high on PCP, I was transferred to the MCJ once again. Somehow they released me that same night with the promise to appear in court. Since I was on felony probation they should not have released me, but I think my sister pulled some strings, having worked at MCJ for a couple of years. The doctors said I was very lucky because not many people come down from overdosing on PCP to be normal again.

I was one of the fortunate ones. A couple of weeks later I was back in jail for a petty theft with a prior, with my second violation and a new case. I was sent to Vacaville State Prison for a ninety day observation to see if I was prison material.

There were a few home boys from the hood at Vacaville who knew me well and their presence made it easier for me to be accepted by the older Norteños and Big Homies. It was here I got my first gang tattoo on my left hand, "XIV Salas." I felt I had earned it. I was just getting settled in when the Big Homies, Shotgun and Conrad, told me there was a child molester in my wing. They told me to deal with him, which I did right after yard recall without getting busted. Later I found out that he was in the Big Homies' wing first and no one had dealt with him; instead they had him moved to the ninety day observation section so I could deal with him. To make a long story short, they used me, rather than doing the work themselves.

For the first couple of weeks I was at Vacaville, the guards had been celling me up with blacks, which I discovered annoyed and irritated me. So while coming back from breakfast one morning I got at the tier officer, explaining to him that though I looked black, I was Mexican and my entire family was Mexican and that I preferred to be celled up with Mexicans. He gave me a stupid look and said out loud for five or six blacks to hear, "What? You don't like blacks? You have a problem with us?" For whatever reason, he tried to cross me up. I quickly explained that the problem was not that I did not like blacks but that I was not black myself and just because I was in prison and looked black did not mean I was going to become black. So with this protest I was celled up with a home boy.

There were a few home boys who did not like me for the simple fact that every Sunday, no matter what was going on the yard, I always went to church to hear Brother Roy, a twenty-five to lifer, preach. He preached the Word with power. No matter how tough one portrayed himself to be, Brother Roy could touch him and stir his spirit. I did not care what certain homies thought, because I knew who I was and that the Lord was still working on me slowly but surely.

After spending three months at Vacaville I was sent back to the county jail. The counselor who interviewed me recommended sixteen months in California Youth Authority (CYA) while the psychiatrist said I was an impulsive person who should not be sent to prison. So these recommendations left me with a fifty-fifty chance of not going to prison. Once back at MCJ the guards placed me in G-pod with Little Man and Z-Bop who were Northern Structure members. While in Vacaville I had heard all the war stories about members of the Northern Structure, how they instilled fear everywhere they went and were straight soldados (soldiers) of the NF.

At county jail all the home boys continued telling me that I was better off going to prison rather than CYA. They thought I was a little knuckle head who would end up getting into more trouble because of all the games going on at CYA. So with their counsel in mind I went to court. The judge called my case and told me he was going to sentence me to sixteen months in CYA. Before he had finished I interrupted and asked him to just go ahead and send me to prison. This decision would prove to be a big mistake on my part.

Now that I as going to the Pinta (prison) I wanted to know everything. Most importantly I wanted to know how to make a shank. Little Man was glad to show me because, as he told me, he and other homies saw some potential in me that could be used to further the "cause" as he referred to it.

Z-Bop and I were on the next bus going to Tracy DVI Prison. Because Z-Bop was well known and since the homies had major influence at Tracy, we were housed in East Hall with all the other homies. I was celled up with a Border Brother from Santa Cruz and there were homies on both sides of me and up and down the tier who showed me love, giving me things I needed. The homie Smokey gave me a quick run down of the program and let me know that there was a Sureño a couple of doors down from me who had been given a pass but was not allowed on the yard. Now acquainted with my surroundings I settled myself in. I soon found out though that, because I had so much time credit, I would not leave the Reception Center but parole from right there in about a month and a half.

The fact that I would be released soon however did not stop me from acting like a fool. The younger homies had been talking about removing the Sureño based on the fact that the Sureños would not give a Norteno a pass if one of us were down south. It was my luck that this Sureño came to my door and asked for my cellie who was sleeping. I do not know if the push-ups I was doing at the time played a factor, but I got up and went off on the Sureño about coming to my door. If he wanted to talk with my cellie, he could wait until he came outside on the tier. This little confrontation would not be the end of it. The next morning while eating breakfast, he gave me a maddog look and said something in Spanish which I could not hear. "Awright," I said, "when we get back to our cells we'll see what's up." My table was released first and I went to my cell and grabbed a piece I had made. Then I went out and stood in front of his cell door. He was halfway up the stairs when he noticed me and then, without hesitation, he quickly turned around and headed downstairs, never to be seen again.

Shortly after this incident the Big Homie Huero came by my cell, looked in and just smiled, shook his head and walked on down the tier. The bad thing about all of this was that I had never used a weapon on anyone. How funny! They sent me to prison at the young age of nineteen in order to teach me a lesson and learn from my mistakes. Yet prison made me worse than when I went in. On September 23rd, 1990 I was paroled from Tracy with orders to report to the local parole office within twenty-four hours or be violated and sent back.

You youngsters now have the deck stacked against you as the courts are locking you up for more lengthy periods of time. Whether you go to prison or CYA, you are serving your sentences among the same corrupted individuals whom you have aspired to become throughout your childhood and adolescence. By sentencing you in this way, society is supplying the minds and bodies that these prison-based gangs need to continue to build and grow. The NF needs youngsters to kill and destroy members of your own Raza, creating more havoc within our communities with much greater intensity than before. You do not even realize that your Big Homies look at you as a two dollar whore to do another man's bidding.

In the past, incarceration of youth for lengthy sentences was the last resort, only when other measures failed or the seriousness of the crime deserved such a punishment. Sadly for you youngsters today, the last resort of the past is now the first resort. The result is that California has one of the world's largest prison systems, with lots of available bed space awaiting you youngsters. There is still lots of barren desert land for new prisons for you if you continue to walk down the road of self-destruction.

Many of you will continue to portray yourselves as if you do not care, acting big and bad as if that is really who you are. Save the drama for some other fool. I have been there and done that and I can tell you that you might as well keep it real with yourselves because you are not fooling anybody but yourselves. Many of you are foolish followers seeking attention, committing stupid, petty crimes or are simply drug addicts, who like myself, might be hardened by imprisonment experiences to go on to commit more serious crimes. The change has to start with you youngsters, here and now.

"Instruct a wise man, and he will be wiser still; teach a righteous man and he will add to his learning" (Proverbs 9:9).

Chapter 7
NORTHERN STRUCTURE: N.R.

I paroled back to Salinas thinking that my sister Patricia would let me stay with her but I had had problems with her husband before I went to prison. Instead she and I went to my tia Carol's house and asked her and her husband to give me a chance by letting me stay there. After some persuasion they decided to give me the benefit of the doubt.

I had come out of prison with a different mentality. I did not want the attention or reputation that I had acquired over the years on the streets. I did not want people to respect me or acknowledge me for being down or a fool; but my past was not going to disappear. No matter how hard I tried to ignore people from my past, I could not shake the picture I had painted in the minds of others.

I attempted to prove to my tio and tia that I was willing to change by taking a job at Taco Bell working nights. A week or two later I got a job working graveyard at Toys-R-Us. The day I was supposed to start working, I loaned my ex-girlfriend, who was my high school sweetheart, my last ten dollars with her promise to pay me back that evening. Before going to work, I went by her house to pick up my ten dollars. Going to her house turned out to be a big mistake on my part. We got into a big argument with some shoving and pushing involved. The last thing I remember was her slamming the door in my face. She really knew how to push my button and as I walked away she opened up the door and yelled that I had gotten burned.

That night at work, I was arrested for attempted robbery, battery and burglary. I had been out exactly one month and found myself once again in MCJ. The charges were finally dropped but I ended up with a seven month straight parole violation and was on the gray goose (parole bus) going back to Tracy DVI prison. The guards took me back to East block and celled me up with old man Huero from San Jose, who had just come back too, after being out for six hours. He was the one who had come by my door last time I was there when I was about to move on that Sureño.

After a few days Huero broached the subject with me about how much I knew about the Northern Structure. I told him I really did not know much, only that they were soldiers for the NF. He asked me if I would like to know more since certain members were asking about me because of the heart I displayed when I was going to deal with the Sureño. He went on to tell me that the NF created the Northern Structure when the administration started locking up the Carnales of the NF. With the Carnales gone, the Norteños were left without protection and guidance from the NF. The EME began to take advantage of this situation, using the Sureños to move on all Norteños or making them pay rent to stay on the mainlines. Because of the rivalries between different towns, there was no unity among Norteños, making it easier for the EME and Sureños to run over the Norteños. So the NF, hearing the cries of the Norteños, composed laws, rules and policies to unite the Norteños together. When some of the Norteños refused to follow the NF's laws, the NF created the Northern Structure which consisted of individuals who were willing to embrace these laws, rules and policies and take a stand for the Norteños who were being abused by the EME. In fact the NF itself was created back in the early sixties to combat abuse by the EME. Actually the name "Northern Structure" was given by the CDC administration.

The real name of this branch was Nuestra Raza (Our Race; the NR) and its members served as soldados or "torpedoes" for the NF to move on any and all EME members.

I remember myself like a little kid, sucking up all this knowledge, fascinated by it all. Since the time I had first come to jail, I had heard about the reputation that the "Salad Bowl" (Monterey County) had in the pinta for being down and straight out fools. Most of the homies from there were NF or NR members. I already had the image in my mind of being a part of this reputation. Huero however went on to say, "Willie, before I point you in this direction I want you to think about all the reasons why you should join and all the reasons why you should not join. If you have any sense whatsoever you will not join because you have more to lose than gain from joining the NR." I wish I would have listened to him because later I would come to regret ever getting involved with the NR or the NF. But in that moment, then and there, all I wanted to be was a part of the gang and feel like I was somebody respected and feared like all the other Big Homies who were hooked up. That weekend at yard I was told to get at the homies Blackneck from Fresno and Gato from Merced. Seeing my willingness, they did not waste time moving me into Gato's cell where I would start my schooling to fully understand my duties and obligations to the NR.

First though they would test me. The day I moved in with Gato he told me about an individual whom I would have to hit at dinner. There was no turning back now. They gave me the shank and pointed out the target. I was to carry out my order as a good little soldier of the NR. Dinner was announced and doors popped. They told me this individual would be leery because he knew he had a green light on him but because I looked black he would not be expecting me. Gato commented that he would think I was his shadow. "Shadow" then became my nickname. But as I moved up behind the guy, he spotted Blackneck and rushed him in front of the officer who started blowing his whistle. The gunner immediately drew down on them, yelling for everyone to get down. About five seconds longer and I would have been putting holes in some guy whom I did not even know nor did I know what he had done. I would have hit this individual simply because I was told to do it in order to prove myself to another man.

Even though I did not get the chance, the homies saw my willingness and accepted me as if I had done it. I was now recruited and married into the Nuestra Raza. The first thing they gave me was what is known as the "NR format," which reads as follows:

"Our future behind the walls depends largely upon each and everyone of us Bros. The will to leave old attitudes to the past and the will to adopt new and more meaningful and fulfilling ideas. The determination to fight and challenge all those who oppose our unity and advancement towards equal justice. Let each of us as Norteños recognize the true purpose of our struggle as a close-knitted Raza.

"Furthermore, let us also be the enlightenment and inspiration for others behind the walls that stand victims to the prejudice and the abuse of the misused authority within the penal system.

"Advancement demands change. It is each Bro's responsibility to promote unity amongst our own kind as well as any other Raza in need of our guidance, assistance or our moral support. A true believer of our struggle is to be treated with dignity and respect on all levels.

"The true purpose and goals of a Bro. behind the walls is to establish a strong positive attitude for himself as well as for the betterment of our Raza and any other minorities in such need. It is apparent that within a Norteño's struggle for better educational opportunities, social respect, and equality, there exist those who are of the same heritage and background who for their own selfish reasons create obstacles and work alongside of other group segments that are contrary to the people's struggle. There is no room whatsoever for the vendidos or any of their kind. Those who seek to destroy and undermine our Raza's efforts to rise above their standards of living have through their own actions made it possible for us and other groups like us to come together, henceforth presenting a strong united front. It is urgent that a Norteño understand his duties and responsibilities and at the same time assert and anticipate the many sacrifices we will all come to endure at one time or another. Many of us will make it to the streets, and some will eventually return, while others will not make it for a very long time and still others will never make it beyond these walls. However, while we are on the inside, we must establish a strong foothold in the pinta for all of those who will remain and those who will return. Our foremost and ultimate goal is to eventually establish a strong front in all the pintas where one is able to do his time and enjoy all the advantages and privileges that make existence behind these walls a more bearable one, while at the same time, expanding one's area of need such as education, vocation, and other necessities essential to our future accomplishments.

"Once firmly established in the pinta, our struggle will gradually expand to the streets. The struggle on the streets will of course be on a much greater scale and will basically follow the same concepts of Nuestra Raza. To fully succeed in our cause, the investment of hard work and time will be much.

"There will be stumbling blocks in the midst of our paths, but through this we shall allow our setbacks to serve us as experience and experience will be the spirit that puts the fire in our hearts and minds for our future accomplishments and victories. To fully accomplish our set goals and objectives, all Bros must function on the same level of awareness of NR rules and regulations adopted for all Bros, as all fronts must function on the same level of awareness and discipline."

When I read the NR format, I could not believe my eyes. After reading this document I believed I had found my true calling. I understood that we were to be the individuals to unite the Raza as we had once been way back before the Raza split between the NF and EME, the North and South. I even asked Gato if this message was the idea the format was conveying to its reader. With a hesitation in his voice, he stated that was one of its purposes. Of course Gato's duty was to recruit me since I was willing, so he told me what I wanted to hear. The main reason I agreed to be a part of the Northern Structure was because it only pertained to life behind the walls. Once a Bro was paroled, he was free of his commitment until he was locked up again.

This idea set well with me because I could do without and wanted no part of a lifetime commitment to the cause outside these walls. Behind the walls was a different world and at stake was either my life or the next man's, victim or victory.

I was led to believe that the NR was the muscle of the NF to protect the Raza from the abuse of the EME so we could do our time in peace and repay all that was done for us in the past by the Carnales of the NF.

After two months, I was called to transpack for transfer to Wasco State Prison. It was a new prison built specifically as a reception center unlike any other. A few days before I was to leave I was given the final rules and laws which I was to abide by for the rest of my life behind walls now that I had committed myself to Nuestra Raza for life. The fourteen bonds were as follows:

"*One*, all Bros will strive for a better education, respect and a social status of equality. This includes and goes beyond acquiring any and all incentives and privileges entitled to an inmate.

"*Two*, all Bros will take a strong, positive attitude towards aiding and assisting all those of Latin descent, as well as any other minority group worthy of our cause. It is our duty to work together in harmony and unite those forces in alliance with us to reach our set goals.

"*Three*, a Bro will do everything in his reach and capability to acquire mainline status, for these are the grounds we must secure for our fellow Norteños and all those who live for the cause to have a strong, established pinta to go to without the threat of interference of the opposition.

"*Four*, in order to continue our struggle with far less obstacles there shall be no tolerance of internal confrontations, individualism or home boy favoritism. No Bro will spread false rumors or negative gossip about a fellow Bro, and at no time will a Bro attempt to take advantage of or disrespect a fellow Bro's ruca or familia. To do so will result in serious repercussions.

"*Five*, all Bros will acknowledge and respect the authority in charge at all times. No Bro will feel inferior to one who holds rank or position. Nor will a Bro holding rank or a position of some type feel superior over his fellow Bros because of his status.

"*Six*, any and all data pertaining to all new arrivals shall be reported through its proper channel immediately (see household procedures), especially that which endangers a life or is contrary to the cause.

"*Seven*, at no time will a Bro endanger the life of a fellow Bro. There shall be no fighting amongst Bros, nor shall any cowardice dealing with the K-9 or enemy be tolerated. To do so will be dealt with accordingly.

"*Eight*, no Bro will lie or boast about his status. Be he rank or file, he will take high regard for his physical and mental well-being and will always strive to better himself and become more aware and educated in all aspects relevant to the accomplishments of our set goals.

"*Nine*, should a Bro be transferred from one facility to another, it is his sole duty to establish a branch in union to procedures set henceforth and work hand-in-hand with other Bros at said facility and parallel with other pintas.

"*Ten*, every chapter and stronghold of Bros will keep track of all enemy activities behind enemy lines.

"*Eleven*, it is each Bro's responsibility who is aware of our struggle to teach and school all those destined for the pinta. No Norteño should enter the pinta blind or without knowledge of our struggle behind the walls.

"*Twelve*, a Bro will protect and defend his household to the fullest, no matter the circumstances or consequences. This means standing next to a fellow Norteño or the cause, both in struggle and battle. To abandon such responsibilities will be considered as an act of treason.

"*Thirteen*, a Bro leaving to the streets is encouraged to assist his fellow Bros behind the walls in whatever form or fashion he may choose. This is not mandatory, but is a step toward the elite circle of dedicated soldados.

"*Fourteen*, a Bro shall stay abreast of all new laws, policies and procedures. No portion of this format is to be misinterpreted or abused for personal gain. To do so will be considered as an act of treason."

These were the laws that would shape the next eight years of my life. I would be in and out of prison, not staying out for more than two months at a time. When I was in prison I was riding to the fullest, catching time and putting in work, taking advantage of young willing Norteños to do the dirty work. Just as the NF felt that they were above us Bros and used us to do their dirty work, so we also looked down upon all Norteños and utilized them.

The truth is I was deceived by this game of manipulation and destruction that continues to destroy our own Raza. Years later I would come to find out that the rules and laws were nothing more than mere words, composed together in order to sound good but obeyed by few. Carnales are sitting up in Pelican Bay SHU serving life sentences and have acquired tens of thousands of dollars on their books, their prison money trust accounts, all through the use of you youngsters whom they use to do their dirty work. Since the late 1990's many of your fellow home boys have been indicted under federal and state charges; yet do you think the Carnales care who gets life or who gets killed because of their financial greed? As long as they are getting their money they do not care whose life is destroyed or lost. The Carnales are playing you brown brothers and sisters for punks and cowards because they make you believe that dropping out is such a bad thing. It is a bad thing for them because they will lose another person whom they cannot control to do their dirty work and bring in more money. They fill your head with lies, rules, laws and policies. They tell you how to feel, how to think and in the process they make you believe you are being "educated." You feel so smart by the time they are done with you but, as a favorite saying of mine goes, "You are so smart that you are stupid."

These laws and rules also deceived me into thinking that there is a difference between providing "data" on individuals and snitching. As long as you are reporting to the Carnales about Snoopy burning Charlie Brown, Pig Pen sleeping with Lucy, the Carnal's old lady, Boo Boo beating up Yogi, Bugs Bunny not paying taxes, Doppy not exercising or Grumpy not doing his five hundred word essay, then you are reporting "info" and "data." Reporting such things through proper channels is acceptable because it is in the best interests of the Carnales and helps them keep track on their stable of fresh meat. I am sorry to bust your bubble you solid soldados but snitching is snitching no matter what they call it. But many of you may not realize this deception because the Carnales have you so blindfolded that you have no idea what you are doing. You become blinded when you allow others to punk you and control you by thinking for you. You see my young brothers and sisters this is brainwashing at its finest.

From the day they recruit a member, the NF begins to teach that individual to kill all those who oppose the NF's interests or stand contrary to their beliefs. Even when there were no enemies and we controlled the pinta, we would start cleaning our own backyard per orders of the Carnales in Pelican Bay SHU. However what the Carnales teach is not what they practice. They are liars. Even though they teach their members to stand by their fellow Carnales closer than blood brothers, yet to date the Carnales of the NF have committed 575 killings of their own kind, other Carnales, NR members and Norteños, far surpassing the killings of their enemies. Furthermore you can take a look at the neighborhoods in Los Angeles and see that the same fact is true for La EME or the Sureños. The real reasons for such bloodshed are internal power struggles and greed among their own members. They do not abide by their own beliefs, laws and constitution. Each person has his own agenda. The NF is a killing machine for the purpose of killing its own kind. I was told before I was recruited that the worst thing about being clicked up is having to hit or move on your own home boys. The EME and NF are one and the same. They are all about destroying their own Raza for their own personal and financial interests.

"A violent man entices his neighbor and leads him down a path that is not good" (Proverbs 16:29).

Chapter 8
BASTA, BASTA!

The only difference between the Nuestra Familia and the Mexican Mafia is that the NF will lie, deceive, and manipulate and even go as far as to force their beliefs on you young brown brothers and sisters. While on the other hand, La EME is straight up with what they are about, which is greed for power, money and drugs.

Both of these gangs are the same in that they will use anyone stupid enough to allow themselves to be used and controlled. These two groups are also the same because they are destroying their own Raza to achieve their selfish goals.

Playing this prison gang game cost me a lot of self-esteem and personal dignity, a price I did not know I had paid until I took a complete inventory of myself, taking an honest look at the things I was doing and the futile life I was living. I had reached the point in my life where I had become tired of exploiting and being exploited. I discovered the truth that we can never really gain from another man's loss.

I will no longer be another man's "toy puppet." I refuse to spend the rest of my life behind these prison walls and give my life for some unworthy cause. I refuse to continue to allow the NF to pimp me by demanding that

I obey and adhere to the Carnales' rules. The NF created these laws for the sole purpose of controlling and deceiving you young people into believing that their ways and their rules actually establish a sense of guidance and direction in the life of a lost soul. I will also be the first to admit that at one time these laws appeared to be very inspirational and full of enlightenment, talking about unity, equality, a better education, and equal justice for La Raza. The words sound good especially to the ears of young people who have had little education or who have experienced some form of physical or mental abuse. These laws are very appealing to youth who never truly felt loved or knew the meaning of love or allowed themselves to be loved. I know that young people, who have had such experiences and who are filled with bitterness and resentment, leave themselves vulnerable to fall for the fallacious ideals of the Carnales and their street gangs.

For over thirty years now, members of these prison gangs have had the audacity to call themselves the "Big Homies" or "Brothers" and claim that their cause is a righteous one for the betterment of their people. The reality is that they have put La Raza on a path of self-destruction with their negative influence. The violence and crime being committed among our gente and the destruction of our own Raza for this so-called "righteous cause," is happening by way of the orders and direction of the Big Homies here in Pelican Bay SHU.

I am certainly not someone important like Padre Hidalgo, Cesar Chavez or Emiliano Zapata, nor am I a Martin Luther King Jr.; but just like them, I will not close my eyes and act as if I do not see the tears in my brothers' and sisters' eyes. I cannot block out their silent cries for help that pierce my ears. I will not pretend as if I do not feel the pain and sorrow of mothers or the hurt and sadness of fathers at seeing their sons' and daughters' lives lost and destroyed because of this foolish madness. I can empathize with the hurt, the loneliness, the emptiness and the sense of betrayal that you young people harbor inside you.

There was a time as a "troubled" youth when I thought I knew it all. I got caught up in the Carnales' prison game, leading to this lonesome prison cell. Locked up inside I began to hear about the Carnales and their cause and struggle. I was fascinated by all the respect and fear everyone seemed to display towards them and by all their enthralling stories. They wanted to impress me so that I would do their dirty work. They still want the same from you youngsters. In the process they will wreck your life as they have wrecked mine. We are like a chain gang of idiots doing the bidding of the NF. If you think for one second that these Big Homies care about you or your life, think again. This is not about peace and unity for La Raza, my brown brothers and sisters. Open your eyes, for "truthful lips endure forever, but a lying tongue lasts only a moment" (Proverbs 12:19).

You young people are foolish if you want to be just like them and carry the title of a Carnal, to make yourself feel special and important, as if you are somebody around your home boys and home girls. But ask yourself, "Who really cares?" Sooner or later you will find that the truth is not what you thought it was. You will see that the "cause" is not worth the sacrifice because it is all just a big lie. By the time you discover or admit the truth it may be too late to escape the trap. Deep in your heart you will be crying out. You will want out. You will want to be with your family, kids, loved ones, and true friends, but because of your foolish desire to be cool and be down, you will have become your Big Homies' fool, just like the Carnales doing life behind these walls. Do you really want to be like them? "The way of a fool seems right to him, but a wise man listens to advice" (Proverbs 12:15).

So please pay heed to my counsel because it is for the good of your future my brown brothers and sisters, so that you will not fill my shoes nor anyone else's for that matter.

Now I am no longer their fool, nor blind to their devious ways. I am tired of being their little punk in a pack, living in the fear of being called "no good" by the Carnales, worrying about what will happen to me if I do not obey their commands. I refuse to let another man, who falsely believes in his own mind that he is some sort of legend, control me as if I am a weak-minded individual.

I will not continue to be their prostitute. In reality a prostitute or hooker is one who sells himself or herself for a low, unworthy purpose. Belonging to the cause of the Carnales is certainly an unworthy purpose. The creation of prison gangs and street gangs alike is for the benefit of another man, just to satisfy his greed and destructive ends. You young people do not have to be prostitutes for the carnales, although, sadly, this is how they feel about you.

Let me share some prison reality with you young people. In prison homosexuals are called "punks" because they are always in need of another man's affection. They allow themselves to be told what to do and when to do it because they are mentally and physically weak. They allow themselves to be taken advantage of, used and abused for another man's personal gain and pleasure. Sadly, these attributes are the same characteristics of so-called soldiers and gangbangers. You must ask yourself, "Whose punk am I today?" If you think you are not someone's punk, then take a look at whose orders you are following, whom you are living for, whom you want to please.

From the perspective of the Carnales and gang members, I am weak, a no good degenerate, a coward, most commonly referred to as a piece of basura (garbage) and sometimes worse. They view me in this way simply because I will no longer obey their orders, do their dirty work and be their "punk" to spend my life behind prison walls because of another man's greed. The Carnales and active members will say the same about you young people who also refuse to be their toy soldier punks. They count on your pride and fear to keep you doing their will. The fact is of course that they are the real cowards and punks living in fear. The Big Homies can trust no one. They have to keep talking to keep their reputation. They have this need to talk bad about others to make themselves look good and feel good. They are the cowards. Someone else does their dirty work for them. When someone calls them a punk or coward they get all hurt inside, feel disrespected and immediately want to fight. Why? Because the truth hurts as we all know.

Their opinion of me is of no importance because I no longer live to please man or gain the acceptance of man. Personally I no longer live in fear of the Carnales or their punks. My actions of moving this pencil across this paper speaks for itself. I intend to keep it real and be real. "For God did not give us a spirit of timidity, but a spirit of power, of love and of self-discipline" (II Timothy 1:7). This power is what I am talking about my brothers and sisters: to be able to stand on your own two feet and do what is right.

The Carnales will tell you my only objective in life is to poison and mislead you young people to do my dirty work, but whose dirty work are you really doing? You are not following my orders or obeying my laws and rules. The Carnales are doing the same ol' song and dance about me as they have about other drop-outs. The fact is I used to say the same things about drop-outs and use the same strategies and tactics in the past when I believed the Carnales' lies.

"Those drop-outs, they're punks, snitches, and cowards with no heart! Don't listen to them; they will deceive you to build a shield of protection around them, because they are no good!" As long as they can keep you full of their blind ignorance and prejudice and keep you unaware of the true purpose of their cause and struggle, then you may think I am a coward. But the reality is that all of us, who have taken a stand to live in peace and be our own individuals, are the brave ones because we do not fear man and refuse to be controlled by man.

The fact is that one has to take the step to be a drop-out, first mentally and then by physical separation from the Carnales' control, in order to see the truth. A person has to step back and look at everything that is going on without being influenced by the pressure of the Big Homies. You have to escape that world of lies to be able to see the truth. As long as you are with those who program you, you will only see the world the way they see it and the way they see it is twisted for their own benefit. They create an image of their world and their enemies only to convince themselves and others that their greed and lust for power is right. They lie to themselves and to others. They lie to you so you will serve them. Do you want to know the truth? Listen to the truth from the outside. You will only be able to accept the truth from the outside but the truth will finally set you free from the lies and deception. Consider the truth, for example, about the history of the NF.

For instance, take a look at the history of the Fresno Bulldogs. The NF Carnales have their own way of telling the story. The Carnales of Nuestra Familia will tell you that in the mid-eighties two of their drop-outs from Fresno poisoned and brainwashed La Gente from Fresno in order to build a shield of protection around themselves. According to the Carnales these two drop-outs used the tactics and concepts that they had been taught by the NF to accomplish this brainwashing of homies against the NF.

I had believed this lie and told this lie for years in order to convince youngsters not to listen to or acknowledge drop-outs. Now that I am a drop-out I have been able to discover the true reason for the creation of the Bulldogs. The NF ordered a Carnal named Crackers to kill a home boy who had been a brother from his youth. As a man of true morals and integrity, he refused and instead started exposing the NF for what they were really all about: greed and power. The truth opened the eyes of many Norteños from Fresno who in turn wanted to have nothing to do with the NF and their so-called "struggles." To stop this fire of truth from spreading to other towns, the NF placed a "green light" on all La Gente from Fresno who refused to obey their rules and policies or do their bidding. The reaction of La Gente in Fresno was to create the gang known as the Fresno Bulldogs in an attempt to protect themselves from the wrath of the NF which was furious from losing a big portion of their stable.

Until this day the NF continues to use Norteños and especially the Northern Structure to persecute Raza from Fresno, especially Bulldogs, to keep them from knowing the truth. Their strategy is to keep you fighting against each other so you will not discover the truth. Sadly the Bulldogs today are becoming just like the NF, after fighting for years not to be like them.

By now many of you should be saying to yourselves, "If the Carnales have lied to us about one part of history, what else have they lied to us about? What is the truth about the NF and La EME? Why are we killing each other for the NF and La EME?" When we were youngsters and just getting involved, we did not even ask such questions. We just blindly believed and followed. Now is the time to find out the truth, all of the truth. You need to know the truth, especially all of you sitting behind these walls for being down for the cause or who have lost loved ones because of the carnales' greed and stupidity.

Throughout my many years of incarceration I have heard numerous accounts and stories of how the so-called "struggle of La Raza" started behind these prison walls. For awhile only members or associates of the NF were the ones telling the story. With each telling of the story, certain details would change, depending on who the storyteller was and how well he could tell a story. In such situations one can only listen and use his own discretion and judgment to separate the facts from the fiction. The most important fact to remember is that those who stand to benefit from twisting the truth are going to tell the story how they want it to be told. The Carnales here in Pelican Bay SHU and the movies "American Me" and "Bound By Honor" are good examples.

I have always considered myself an open-minded person and have often wondered what kind of stories the Carnales of La EME tell their Sureños. I also have been curious to know their side of the story to compare it to what the NF told me. My tia always told me, "Willie, there are always two sides to every story." My problem was that she never wanted to hear my side of the story, I have to admit, with good reason.

Now that I am my own man, I have finally had the opportunity to speak with a couple of ex-Mexican Mafia members as well as ex-Nuestra Familia members, who now have nothing to gain or benefit from their stories. In doing so, I have satisfied my curiosity because now I have a clear understanding of what actually went down, thanks to my brown brothers who have kept it real. I have received the true story from both sides. All agree that those who began La EME and NF were just a bunch of blind, ignorant fools promoting a dope fiend's cause.

Unfortunately I was also their fool because I was a part of this struggle of stupidity. Now you can know the truth because, unlike in the past, now many want to hear what those Carnales did not want us to know, history that they themselves would not talk about because it reminds them of how ignorant they really were. Here is the history as it unfolded without the distortions of the Carnales who only see what they want to see and who refuse to face the truth. From the true history you will see why they despise drop-outs.

In the late 1950s in California's Department of Corrections no particular race dominated over the rest, or suppressed the others, nor did one group have control of the prison or its yards. Aside from the everyday personal conflicts and racial tension between whites and blacks, everyone was more laidback and minded their own business, doing their own thing.

It was a world in which drugs were an essential part of life. Drugs predicted the type of atmosphere hanging over the prison yards, which could change from peace and harmony to war and hatred in a blink of an eye over a twenty-dollar bag of dope. Those who could control the import and distribution of drugs in the prison also controlled the prison. The inevitable combination of drugs and money brought power and control.

In 1958, the Mexican Mafia began in Folsom State Prison as nothing more than a cluster of "Tecatos" (heroin addicts) who perceived the profits one could acquire by controlling the drug market behind the walls. Over a period of years La EME grew strong in numbers. They had created a Tecato's dream. They were able to get high and stay high 24/7 in prison despite the fact that the quantity of drug purchased was smaller and the price was far more expensive than the outside world.

La EME's objectives were simple enough. First and foremost they wanted to take control of the flow of drugs coming into the prison, so all members could profit and most importantly use and abuse any drug of their preference. They also wanted to be able to live a lavish lifestyle as best as one could while doing time behind the walls. In addition they wanted to be recognized by all as gangsters, establishing themselves as the most powerful prison gang in California.

They became well known for extortion, killing, rape and taking advantage of their own kind. From La EME's point of view, if you were not EME, you were "nada" (nothing). Anyone or anything they could use in order to gain profit for themselves was at the mercy of these Carnales. Those who refused to comply with La EME's demands were quickly dealt with. Violence of course was the means La EME used to make its statements. The significance of violent acts was easily understood by all: the power of fear! They continue to use the same power of fear today to control and profit from the gente caught up in gangs behind the walls and outside the walls, especially throughout Southern California.

The Mexican Mafia became powerful and wealthy, establishing themselves on the streets of Los Angeles since the majority of its members were from there. However only those members from East LA, the leaders and founders along with a few others, were prospering while everyone else was getting kibbles and bits, doing all the dirty work. This imbalance of profits created envy, jealousy and hatred within La EME and its members, leading a few Carnales from Southern California to drop out of La EME and to begin secretly plotting to overthrow what La EME had established.

In 1963, these drop-out Carnales secretly began to organize La Raza under false pretenses. Since La EME was so strong, controlling just about every prison, it took years for these drop-outs to build a gang strong enough to stand up against La EME. Throughout those years the abuse and mistreatment by La EME continued, which worked out to the advantage of the ex-Carnales. The former EME Carnales exploited the abuse of La EME along with support for the Chicano Movement and La Causa of Cesar Chavez to extend their own influence. They wanted to motivate La Raza from the north, who were also referred to as farmeros, many of whom, unlike La Gente from the south, had not grown up in gangs. The ex-EME Carnales also promoted their so-called "People's Struggle" among gente from the south as well as those who had not been EME members. They claimed to be for the people and imposed strict rules and laws on their members. They were well organized, disciplined and very militant. They even went so far as to implement a no-drug use policy. Many of La Raza truly believed that this new cause was a righteous one for the betterment of La Gente. It all sounded and looked so good, supposedly the opposite of La EME. This beginning was the apparently innocent start of Nuestra Familia but the reality was that the leadership of the NF was really interested in the drugs and profit that La EME leadership would not share.

In 1968, a Carnal from La EME stole a pair of shoes from a Carnal of the NF, which had become a force to be reckoned with by this time. Unknown to this EME member at the time, his action was to be the straw that broke the camel's back.

On September 16th, 1968, when the Mexican Mafia was celebrating Mexico's Day of Independence, Nuestra Familia declared war with the element of surprise, supposedly for the betterment of La Raza to stop all the abuse, at least so they led La Raza to believe!

Soon the whites, allying with the Carnales of La EME, began the Aryan Brotherhood. The blacks allied with the Carnales of the NF and started the Black Guerrilla Family. The war continued for years in all prisons before NF members realized they had all been deceived. By then it was too late because too much blood had been spilled on both sides. The war had become a matter of pride, power, drugs, and money. The very first Carnales of the NF had planned from the beginning to take over all that La EME had established and within a couple of years the NF had become exactly like La EME! Yes my young brothers and sisters, La Nuestra Familia was in fact created by a bunch of drop-outs from La EME! The NF hates drop-outs because they were created by drop-outs and they fear the truth.

In the mid 70's the California Department of Correction's administration and the Governor of California began locking up all gang members in the hole (SHU) for indeterminate sentences, deeming them threats to the safety and security of inmates and the institutions. In the hole La EME began poisoning the mind of La Raza from the south in order to keep their Tecato's dream alive. They claimed their cause as the cause of La Gente. They created the Sureños, their toy punk soldiers, to carry out their orders and provide them with their drugs. The Sureños became tools to keep La Gente from the south in check and under the EME's influence through force and fear in order to continue to fight against the NF. These movements began the split among La Raza, with Bakersfield, California being the borderline between the Norte (North) and the Sur (South). Gangs had been a part of life for La Raza from the Sur so the EME's job of intimidation and control in the south was easy.

Just like La EME was controlling the La Raza in the south, the NF attempted to do the same thing with La Raza from the Norte. But when some members of La Raza would not submit, the NF created the "Northern Structure" or "Nuestra Raza" (NR), which was its real name, to exercise broader power and influence. Members of the NR were to be the soldiers of the NF with the promise of becoming Carnales themselves. The NR, of which I was a member, was used to promote the NF's ways and beliefs among La Raza from the Norte and to guarantee that the Carnales could do their time in peace behind the walls, without the threat of La EME.

Now the Northern Structure (NR) has been disbanded, because of the ongoing power struggles in Pelican Bay SHU among the Carnales. In addition the "Hermanos" as we were called in the NR also grew tired of the deceit. When the Carnales saw they were losing power and respect from NR Hermanos and many of them were dropping out, the Carnales began giving the bonds and format to all Norteños, the young street soldiers, in order to use the Norteños against ex-Northern Structure members. These laws were forced on all Norteños and those who refused to abide by them were hit or deemed no good. The Carnales are still trying to stop the truth from getting out by using Raza against Raza.

What are you, my brown brothers and sisters, fighting and killing each other for? You are fighting just to protect the power of the Carnales. Their profit and power is the only "cause" and "struggle." This "struggle" is destroying La Raza. La Raza cannot even study their own culture or history or have any artwork of La Raza, because it has all been exploited and devalued by the Carnales of both gangs. Any gente found to be in possession of material representing the cultural history of La Raza are deemed gang members or associates of La EME or the NF, depending on where they are from. La Raza suffers from the ignorance of the Carnales who claim they want to protect La Raza. Whether they are NF or EME, they are both one and the same, Tecatos and Tecatos in denial, committing genocide against their own gente.

To all Sureños, who are the Mexican Mafia's prostitutes claiming Sur and flagging all that blue like a bunch of "blueberry suckers on a stick," killing each other and fighting against Norteños, go ahead and keep the zapatos and let those dope fiend Carnales fight their own war and support their own drug habit. "Basta mi Raza!"

And to all you Norteños being prostituted by the Nuestra Familia, killing each other and warring against Sureños, claiming Norte, and sporting all that red like a bunch of "strawberry suckers on a stick," forget about the zapatos and let your dope fiend Carnales fight their own bogus cause and support themselves. "Basta mi Raza!"

And to all you Raza who continue to be "punks" for these Carnales, when you finally reach the pinnacle of your futile career, and you are sitting here in Pelican Bay SHU for the gang, do not forget to ask the Carnales for those zapatos, which you threw your whole life away for!

Now it is time to keep it real mi young Raza, as a gang member you have no real courage, heart, or love. You are cowards and act out of fear. You will quickly pick up a knife and stab someone in the back or pick up a gun do a drive-by or gang up and jump someone. There is only one percent who will stand up like real men and women for the other ninety-nine percent. If you were by yourself with no weapon in hand and on equal terms face to face, you could not fight your way out of a wet paper bag, and would only bust a grape after rounding up your homies to back you up. You're nothing more than cowardly bullies who need a gun or a knife or your homies to make you feel strong, special and important. Now you must find the heart and courage to be you own individual.

One thing I have come to realize about the majority of the Carnales is that they cannot fight worth a lick one on one and this is the reason why they are Carnales: they need to use others to do their fighting for them. They are cowards themselves. As they say, "Cowards run in packs."

In the 1980s, news networks throughout California were covering the gang wars going on between the Crips and the Bloods. African Americans were killing their own kind behind a color of a rag and a town or street they were from, the majority of the minority at that time committing genocide against their own kind. A call for a truce and peace began to be heard in the streets, ending the gang wars, though not before the movie "Colors" was made, glorifying gang life. The movie ended with La Raza getting into a shoot-out and being arrested. How ironic!

Today there exists a different majority among the La Raza minority: the

Sureños and Norteños who have filled the shoes of the Crips and Bloods. Now it is La Raza who are on the network news and newspapers. "American Me" and "Bound By Honor" only glorified "la vida loca." "Basta Basta!" My young brothers and sisters, we need to open our eyes and learn from the mistakes and history of our African brothers and sisters. Some day the Sureños and Norteños will call a halt to the violence and then we will ask again, "Why did we commit so much bloodshed? What was the purpose?" There will be no reasonable, rational explanation for so many deaths and destruction.

If we do not reveal the truth, then there will be more violence, crime and destruction among our Raza, destroying many more families and creating more chaos and madness within our communities. If these Carnales here in Pelican Bay SHU truly believe that I am going to lie down and go away like so many others of the past, they are sadly mistaken and are going to be very disappointed. I know all about their examples and statements of violence designed to pump fear into the hearts of you young people who refuse to bow down to them and follow their orders, or any of you who dare to tell the truth or speak about them in a negative manner. Basta!

I now stand here today as a warrior of the Lord and "*eagerly expect and hope that I will in no way be ashamed but will have sufficient courage so that now as always Christ will be exalted in my body, whether by life or by death. For to me, to live is Christ and to die is gain*" (Philippians 1:20-21).

Chapter 9
THE WAY, THE TRUTH AND THE LIFE

On New Years eve 1998 I decided to drop out of the gang. I decided that by dropping out, although I would lose the respect I once had, perhaps everyone would just leave me alone. I was sick and tired of the ongoing power struggles between Carnales in prison that were causing murders, left and right, of good home boys on the streets. The Carnales in C-facility and D-facility in Pelican Bay SHU were having meaningless disputes and these conflicts were leading to deaths on the streets. Later in August of 1999 before I was paroled from Pelican Bay SHU, I was housed in C-facility 6 Block. At that time the Carnal Mateo, who was doing life, told me to tell all the homies in the Salinas Regiment that everyone was all good and all the problems were just a big misunderstanding. I could not believe the words I was hearing from him. Many good home boys were killed, assaulted, sliced and deemed no good, and now the Carnales had the nerve to say it was all just a misunderstanding. "Basta!"

Throughout my many years of being involved in the gang, I have seen many assaulted, stabbed, and killed by the orders of these Carnales over petty reasons or for no reason at all. So much of the violence originates from their personal vendettas and internal power struggles with members of their own gang here in Pelican Bay SHU. They want to try to prove who has the most power and influence among them over you young people. These battles and wars are fought out in the streets and in other prisons by you young people involved in gangs. You are their sacrificial pawns they use to amuse themselves. They sit here in peace and safety in the SHU with the same individuals and enemies whose soldiers they convince you to fight and die fighting. To these Carnales in their prison cells, the war is a game to entertain themselves during their boredom; to you it is a matter of life and death. "Basta!"

As a result of the Carnales' games, many of you youngsters out on the streets will be indicted, convicted and end up behind walls, even adding more years to your sentence, in some cases life terms, if you continue to play the games. You will pay the ultimate sacrifice in addition to committing murder for them. What is the purpose? The purpose is not to defend La Raza. La Raza is being destroyed. The purpose is for the entertainment of the Carnales. "Basta, mi Gente!"

Both the NF and La EME are facing desperate times today because so many are dropping out now after seeing the truth, realizing that the only thing one has to look forward to is life in prison or death. For the past few years they have been recruiting every ignorant young or old person who comes through prison and on the streets with the promise of one day making them a Carnal. Wow! Life in prison or dead. All these efforts are an attempt to keep their name alive and use you ignorant blind fools to sell their drugs, do their dirty work, and force their beliefs on you younger brown brothers and sisters out in the streets. "Basta, Basta mi Raza!"

Fortunately there have been overwhelming numbers of young and old gente alike who have come to their senses, dropping out of the gang before it is too late. There are even more who are doing long prison sentences and even life, who have also dropped out, realizing that they have ruined their lives for another man's gain.

"Say to them, 'As surely as I live, declares the Sovereign Lord, I take no pleasure in the death of the wicked, but rather that they turn from their ways and live. Turn! Turn from your evil ways! Why will you die, O house of Israel?" (Ezekiel 33:11)

My brown brothers and sisters and all others who might be the next victims of the Big Homies and the gang, let my ignorance and my past foolish mistakes as well as those of others serve as experience to open your eyes. Let the destructive experience of others be the inspiration and enlightenment that ignites the fire within your heart and mind for future accomplishments.

"Trust in the Lord with all your heart and lean not on your own understanding; in all your ways acknowledge him, and he will make your paths straight" (Proverbs 3:5–6).

Mi Raza, we must all come together as one body and one voice to be heard. We all have to take responsibility to successfully eliminate and eradicate the works of this "brood of vipers " and these "parasites" that plague our gente and spread their vile influence throughout our communities. We have to fight, not through violence, but through education, knowledge and by simply refusing to be used and abused by these Carnales and the gang. These vipers thrive on the sweat and blood of their own people's hard work and seek to destroy our younger brothers and sisters' lives for their own selfish reasons. Within our communities we must eliminate any possibility whatsoever for the Carnales or any of their kind to oppose peace, unity and advancement towards equality for all nuestra Raza!

As I write to you young men and women, my words are straight and blunt so that you will understand exactly how the Carnales are playing you. I hope you will not misunderstand my words because love and compassion motivate me to write to you, mi Gente. I know for certain that because of this message of truth, the Carnales will be very anxious to seek my life. Nevertheless, I will not run from them nor will I hide from them. I do not hate them because many of them were like us at one time or another, lost and blinded by Satan's darkness, allowing their pride and ignorance to destroy their lives and the lives of their own people. Therefore, I will pray for these Carnales regardless of their hatred towards me. The Lord has given us this command: "Whoever loves God must also love his brother" (1 John 4:21).

If you my young brothers and sisters have naively absorbed and gullibly accepted the false theories and ideologies of others who want to take advantage of you, remember that in the long run those human rules and theories end in misery and death. Proverbs 14:12 says, "There is a way that seems right to a man, but in the end it leads to death." Do not lose heart my brothers and sisters, there is a way for all of you who are tired of living in fear and worry; tired of being a follower and tired of having to depend on gangs, homies, drugs, and alcohol to make you feel good, strong and whole inside. Jesus Christ is, "the way, the truth, and the life" (John 14:6).

For thirty years I thought I was somebody, selling dope and caught up in la vida loca as a so-called "gangster" but at the right time, at the age of thirty-six, God has shown me that I am nothing without Him. As I sat in Santa Cruz County Jail, back inside after having been out for just a little more than twenty days, feeling like a complete failure and loser, coming down hard off drugs and alcohol, I was looking around the cell for a place to tie my sheet and hang myself and at the same time crying out to God for help. As I looked around that cell God spoke to my heart and let me understand that if I would put Him first in my life, before anyone or anything else, then He would give me what my heart desired. Matthew 6:33 sums up the Lord's promise: "But seek first his kingdom and his righteousness, and all these things shall be given to you as well."

Since then He has stripped me of my foolish pride. He took away my so-called "bad ass" reputation, my selfishness and all my self-righteousness. All these years I have lived for the honor and praise of men and the materialistic things of this world. I have been a failure and a disappointment to myself, to my family and especially my daughter. But Jesus says: "I have come that they may have life and have it to the full" (John 10:10). And it is through the blood of Jesus that I have been given a second chance in life and have been forgiven of all my sins for His great name's sake. He has set me free of all my hurt, pain and sorrow; and has filled me with His joy, love, comfort and peace which surpasses all understanding.

"Therefore, if anyone is in Christ, he is a new creation; the old has gone, the new has come" (2 Corinthians 5:17).

You young people must decide for yourselves, whether you are going to continue to follow Satan down his path of destruction which leads to death, or if you are going to trust in Jesus and follow Him down that straight and narrow path that leads to life. How many of you today have the heart and courage to say enough is enough, I'm tired of being another man's punk and prostitute, tired of being used, abused and taken advantage of, tired of destroying my life and the lives of my own people? How many of you are tired of hurting, and feeling empty inside? How many of you are tired of being a failure and a disappointment to your family, children, and loved ones?

In life we must decide our own destiny. God's greatest gift to His children is the free will to choose their own path in life. But you must think about the consequences of your decisions and understand what lies ahead on the path you choose to walk in life. Do not let other men do your thinking for you. Grow up and think for yourself. Live for the honor of your parents and children who in the end are going to be the only ones there for you.

"See, I set before you today life and prosperity, death and destruction. For I command you today to love the Lord your God, to walk in his ways, and to keep his commands, decrees and laws; then you will live and increase…This day I call heaven and earth as witnesses against you that I have set before you life and death, blessings and curses. Now choose life so that you and your children may live (Deuteronomy 30:15–16, 19).

EPILOGUE

"Enter through the narrow gate. For wide is the gate and broad is the road that leads to destruction, and many enter through it. But small is the gate and narrow the road that leads to life, and only a few find it" (Matthew 7:13–14).

In the summer of 2000, I was arrested on numerous drug charges and battery on a peace officer and given a seven year prison sentence. While in the county jail in a drop-out pod, I began reading the Bible and trying to make sense of my life and life in general. During this period of time that I spent looking inside myself and thinking about my purpose, I noticed all the new young faces who were now taking the place of all the older homies who also happened to be with me in the same pod. Seeing the young ones trying to fill the shoes of the older ones convinced me to try to warn these youngsters, especially since my little cousin was in the active pod right next door. My conscience started playing with me because my little cousin was caught up in this prison gang and his little brothers were following right behind all of us. I was to blame in part because I had influenced them and schooled them when I was active in the game. Now that I was no longer a part of that game, if something were to happen to them, like catch a life sentence or be killed, my conscience would eat me alive.

So I began to write a newspaper article with the hope of enlightening you youngsters now caught up. Once I had finished the article it was too long to be printed as a newspaper article. Furthermore I wanted the article to have wider coverage than just one day in the newspaper. When I left county jail for prison I was determined to put something together to open the eyes of many youngsters. While in Delano State Prison I ran into an ex-Sureño with ninety-five years to life who was writing a book about his life experience with the gang. I decided to turn this newspaper article into a book and thought about all the money I would make. I was transferred to Corcoran State Prison SHU and started writing, but each time I tried to write, I found that I could not express myself. So I decided to put the book idea aside and just focus on reading and studying God's word. The more I read, the more life began to have meaning. I realized that Jesus Christ had given His life for me and you so that we would not have to live a life of sin, leading to destruction. Jesus Christ was the one who could take away all my pain, hurt and tears of thirty years. Jesus filled me with a peace that I had never felt. Drugs, women, crime and the gang did not even come close to this peace which now rules my heart. Just as Jesus Christ gave His life for me, I wanted to give my life to Him and I committed my book to be used to open the eyes of others. No longer was I going use this book to make money. It was no longer about the money, but about the message. When I tried to write again the words just flowed and I thank God for that because now I was writing for the right purpose.

I came to be on fire for the Lord, reading anything I could get my hands on so I could obtain as much knowledge and wisdom as possible from God rather than man. Soon I was transferred to Pelican Bay Prison SHU to do the remainder of my time. I finished my book and continued to read the Word and grow closer to the Lord. Four months before I was scheduled to parole I was placed in the Mainline Transitional Housing Unit. During my stay there I met ex-EMEs, ex-Sureños, ex-Aryan Brothers, ex-NF, ex-Norteños. We all had the same story and understood of how ignorant we were to sacrifice our lives for a bunch of ignorant homies serving life sentences.

I will never forget the story of the homie Richard from down south, an ex-Carnal of La EME, who at the age of eighteen in the early 70s came to San Quentin for a simple marijuana charge. He got caught up however with La EME and in order to be accepted by the gang committed murder, turning a three year sentence into a life sentence. What was the purpose? For over twenty years he had dedicated his life to La EME, not even thinking of his family. In 2000, when he received a picture of his family, his mom, tias and tios, sadly he could not even recognize his mom anymore. Reality hit him deep and hard. He had thrown his whole life away and put his family last before the homies. That picture convinced him at age forty-seven to come to his senses and drop out of the gang.

There are so many stories of home boys like Richard and to write about them would take many chapters. How long will it take for you youngsters to come to your senses? Will you wait ten, twenty or thirty years into your life sentence for the Carnales and then realize you have been used and that you have thrown your life away? The fact that we all got along so well on this yard blew my mind. We set our differences aside because they were false differences that the gangs had instilled in our minds and hearts. We all had determined to be our own individuals instead of being another man's punk. When we first went to prison we thought we would never be anyone's punk but then we got caught up following laws and rules that served only to make us another man's punk. So you youngsters can use this book and the experiences of others to avoid falling into the same trap. You have the choice. You do not have to listen to me. You can learn for yourselves and after you are locked up with big time for serving the whims of the carnales, you can kick yourselves because you did not heed God's warnings. I am just the messenger whom God has chosen to open up your eyes and ears, to see and listen.

For ten years I believed the Carnales and thought that what I was doing would one day bring peace for our gente. It was a lie. There is no peace for the Raza except among the Carnales themselves in Pelican Bay SHU. So do you youngsters still believe this is a struggle for the betterment of La Raza? During thirty-nine years of existence, how has the Carnales' cause been better for our Raza? How many Sureños and Norteños have been killed for this cause? How many are doing long terms in prison for this cause? If you serve the Carnales' cause you can expect one out of three things to happen in your life: you can end up dead, you can end up with life or you can drop out, enjoy life and live. What will you choose? It is your choice.

While I was on that yard, I never believed that I would see mi gente living together in peace and harmony on a mainline yard, in the same cells together, eating together, playing football, basketball and handball together and just being men without trying to control one another. I never thought harmony would be possible. Peace has happened but not as a result of the Carnales' beliefs or ways. The only way to have true peace is to separate yourself from the Carnales' game and live a life according to Jesus Christ.

After dropping out I did two years and eight months as a dedicated soldier of the Lord. I did not care what others thought about me or said about me. My aim was to please the Lord and Him only. One day when I went to yard, I started thinking of my mom and what she must have endured the last days of her life, the pain, hurt, and suffering. Memories of her brought tears to my eyes, but then I suddenly understood what God's Son Jesus Christ had to endure the last days of His life. I then realized that what my mom endured was nothing compared to what Jesus Christ endured for us all. Right then and there my pain and tears for my mom were wiped away and I began to praise the Lord for everything in my life, the good and the bad. Satan wanted to turn my life into some evil purpose, but the Lord turned it into something good. I would not exchange my life in the Lord for anything. I would not give it up for the world.

That time I served allowed me to see and know God in an intimate way.

I came to understand why God had allowed everything to happen in my life. I have made many mistakes in my life and many family members, friends and loved ones have given up on me. My daughter was taken away from me and at this moment she is filled with resentment and anger towards me because of the life I have lived. But I know that as long as I seek God's kingdom first, He will add everything else to me. God has led me through life for His purpose and plan to reach out to all those who have experienced what I have gone through in life. I feel so privileged to be called and chosen for His kingdom's work. If losing everything that I hold dear must happen, so be it for everything of this world is temporary; but the kingdom of God is everlasting. You youngsters must ask yourselves the question, "Do I want a life that is temporary and without purpose or do I want a life that is everlasting with true purpose and meaning?"

"I would rather be a doorkeeper in the house of my God than dwell in the tents of the wicked. For the Lord God is a sun and shield; the Lord bestows favor and honor; no good thing does he withhold from those whose walk is blameless" (Psalm 84:10-12).

In January of 2003 I paroled from Pelican Bay Transitional Housing, certified as a NF/NR gang drop-out. I truly felt that I was prepared to finally get my life together by living a life with Christ Jesus. I was on fire for the Lord and felt that I would never go back to my old ways. But never say never because even the apostle Peter said he would go to death with Jesus and then ended up denying three times that he even knew Jesus, just as Jesus had predicted. I had asked God for guidance and strength to overcome the temptations of the world. Before I paroled I prayed and asked God for wisdom and protection from repercussions from the gang and to use my book in a mighty way. The problem was that I had not given Him my whole heart.

God is so good and is just waiting with open arms for us to ask Him to help us in this crazy world. I was not out more than a week when I read in the newspaper that the Carnales and their toy soldiers had just been arrested on drug charges and conspiracy to commit murder. If I had been worried, I was worried no more. It felt good to hear people say I had changed so much. God was guiding me and giving me strength to overcome temptation. This time out was the first time in my fourteen years of doing time that I did not come out using drugs or drinking on that first day. God had taken that desire away. All I wanted to do was share Jesus with everyone I came across.

After three months though I started allowing myself to slip and rather than waiting on the Lord I started looking for that special woman that I had asked God for. During my search I started neglecting the basics of God's word. I got a job at a moving company with a home boy I grew up with and before I knew it I was smoking cigarettes which only opened the door to other things. I stopped going to church and fellowship and began sleeping around with women looking for that special woman. I should have realized that God was not going to bless me with a woman while I was living in sin. Finally I started messing around with a woman involved in drugs and before long I was back into my old ways headed down that road of destruction.

Within a month I quit my job and was selling drugs. I was neck deep in la vida loca once again. I stopped going around mi familia and even stopped seeing my daughter. I used the excuse that I did not want her to see me on drugs, but the truth was that I was embarrassed about the lifestyle I had fallen back into. After doing so good while I was walking with Jesus, I allowed myself to return to the same old miserable life that Jesus Christ had just pulled me out of. I gave up a life of peace for a life of problems. After I separated myself from God my whole life crumbled. My car broke down; I got in debt; the parole officer was on me; my family became disappointed in me; and in order to relieve my conscience I stayed high and dealt drugs. The greatest mistake was that I left the shadow and protection of the Almighty, I had placed myself in the hands of Satan once again; "a thief comes only but to steal and kill and destroy."

On October 27th, 2003 about 1:00 AM while coming out of my good friend's house to meet some girl, I was confronted by another girl and a guy. As I walked toward them the girl moved out of the way and the guy began unloading on me. Fortunately for me this guy seemed more scared than I was. One bullet only grazed my knee and another bullet went straight through my calf. This guy must have fired eight to twelve shots at me and had me dead to rights since I was no more than ten to fifteen feet in front of him and walking towards him. From my point of view he should have finished the job because now I was going to show those two what time it was. By the next evening I knew their names and addresses. Since I was on the run from parole I could not go to the hospital. I needed a place to lay low and remembered that a woman I had met before I started backsliding named Lisa had gotten her own place. So I gave her a call and explained what happened. She said I could stay with her. So that day I moved in with her, but I did not even slow down. I just dropped my belongings off and was on my way, running around town selling dope.

I was so caught up in Satan's snares I did not even realize that God was trying to get my attention to turn from my sinful ways; but I did not get His message from the bullet holes in the leg. The day after I was shot I was riding around at night, going by the places where these people hung out, just looking for someone to take vengeance on or someone to send a message back to the Carnales that they were coming for the wrong guy. But God has a way of getting our attention, especially for those whom He has a plan and a purpose for in life. A few nights later I was at my friend George's house and we started talking about who shot me. George was white could not understand who shot me. As I was explaining to him about my prison gang involvement and that now I was a drop-out, I remembered, by explaining everything to him, that I had dropped out of the gang. Then I also realized at that moment that I was on a mission of revenge which would only lead me to kill someone and receive a life sentence because of the gang and the Carnales. I would defeat the purpose of dropping out. Instead of getting revenge and killing these two people who were just punks being used to do another man's dirty work, I decided I needed to finish what I had begun. I thought that I should return to writing my testimony and hopefully do some major damage by exposing the Carnales for what the really are, degenerates and parasites!

On November 1st, 2003 I was arrested on numerous charges, including a gun charge and sales charge. As soon as I was housed and rested I realized God had once again saved me through His amazing grace and mercy. I knew God had placed me back in jail to finish what I had started. I immediately got started on my book again and began rewriting it. It is my belief that God has a special plan for those of us who are locked up because behind the walls God can try to get our attention. When we are out in the world we get so caught up in all the negativity that we do not have time to seek God or even call upon His Son's mighty name. The cares of the world choke out the cares of God's kingdom.

Many of us are caught up in the ways of the world. We focus on things that make us feel good and look good to impress other people. We never have time for God nor are we interested. We are lured away by our own desires, and deceived by the evil one. "For everything in the world—the cravings of sinful man, the lust of his eyes and the boasting of what he has and does—comes not from the Father but from the world" (1 John 2:16).

So to all my brothers and sisters doing time, I say thank God for His loving kindness, mercy and grace that He grants you. Rather than leaving you out in a world of confusion and on a path of destruction that would lead to death, you may be locked up with the time and motivation to examine yourself spiritually and to mediate on your purpose in life. Until you realize God is calling you and until you answer that call, expect to keep coming back behind those walls. To all of you who keep getting into trouble and struggling in life, feeling miserable all the time, having to stay high just to feel some peace of mind, God is calling and is waiting for you to call upon Him.

I pray you young brothers and sisters will pay heed to the counsel of those who have gone before you and who have seen the truth, chosing the path of righteousness. Do not fall victims to the games of the NF/Norteños or La EME/Sureños. Remember you have nothing to prove to anyone but yourself and God. The choice is yours. Do not let others make your choices for you. Be your own man, not a punk two dollar whore for another man.

I have composed a list in hopes of helping you decide where you want your path in life to take you. The following are those I have done time with and those who have crossed my path behind the walls. All have been a part of a prison gang and the Carnales' game of "La Causa." There are two groups. Will you be in one of them? You must decide where you are going.

Albert "Beto" Avilla	murder victim
Alfonso "Pachie" Alvarez	murder victim
Andora Russo	murder victim
Anthony "Tony" Florez	murder victim
Arthur "Art" Florez	murder victim
Barry San Jose	murder victim
Darin "Smiley" Hardin	murder victim
Eli Rosas	murder victim
Estaban Guzman	murder victim
Esther Alvarez	murder victim
Federico Arevalo	murder victim
Geronimo Garza	murder victim
Hector Padilla	murder victim
James Walter Brown	murder victim
Jesse Renteria Castro	murder victim
Johnny Sococie	murder victim
Jose "Joe' Banvelos	murder victim
Marcos Baca	murder victim
Michael "Mikeo" Castillo	murder victim
Paul Farfan	murder victim

Ray "Chocolate" Perez	murder victim
Robert "Brown Bod" Viramontes	murder victim
Rosemary "Rosie" Levas	murder victim
Rudolpho "Cheyene" Cadena	murder victim
Sheila Apodaca	murder victim
Tony "Little Weasel" Herrera	murder victim
Victor "Victorio" Murillo	murder victim
Richard "Big Rich" Hagler	strangled by cellmate

These individuals thought they were somebody and wanted to prove their loyalty and honor to the Carnales. At one time they were deemed solid soldados, worthy brothers and sisters, but because of jealousy, envy, hatred, and personal agendas their reward was death. Death was their reward for years of dedication to the Carnales and the gang. The majority of these individuals were killed by their own trusted gang members. So you see mis Hermanos y Hermanas, the amount of work you put in for them does not matter, for when you are used up and washed up they will not hesitate to add you to this list. Basta mi Raza!

Vincente "Polukas" Altamoreno	life in prison
Vincente "Che" Arroyo	25 years to life in prison
Sheldon "Skip" Villanueva	15 years in prison
Santos "Bad Boy" Brunas	50 years to life in prison
Rudy "Dancing Bear" Miramontez	life in prison
Ronnie "Lucky" Shelton	100 years to life in prison
Robert "Robot" Salas	life in prison
Robert Lee Mares	40 years in prison
Robert "Cracker" Vindiola	life in prison
Richard "RB" Cagadas	25 years to life in prison
Paul "Spokio" Salcido	102 years in prison
Patrick "Chino" Smith	65 years in prison

Pablo "Polie" Rodriguez	10 years in prison
Negro from Gilroy	life in prison
Miguel "Little Blackie" Garza	13 years in prison
Matthew "Mateo" Rocha	27 years to life in prison
Juan Padilla	life in prison
Jose "Blondie" Gonzales	life in prison
Joseph "Pinky" Hernandez	life in prison
Jerry "Chino" Hernandez	sentenced to death
Jerry "Crippled Jerry" Salazar	25 years to life in prison
James "Huevo" Trujeque	sentenced to death
James "Conejo" Perez	life in prison
James Blanco	40 years in prison
Isidro "Chilo" Huerta	10 years in prison
Herminio "Spankio" Serna	sentenced to death
Hecto "Copas" Gallegos	20 years in prison
Glen "Hobo" Holden	life in prison
Fidel "Boxer" Delariva	life in prison
Enrique "Rica" Galvan	18 years to life in prison
Edward "Parajo" Vargas	60 years in prison
Edward "Eddie" Feliciano	sentenced to death
Donald "Wino" Perez	life in prison
Dion Garzagolla Jr.	25 years to life in prison
David "Rock" Ramirez	life in prison
David "Pontiac" Garcia	life in prison
David "Joker" Ramirez	20 years in prison
David "DC" Cervantez	life in prison
Darin "Smiley" Hardin	murder victim
Ceasar "Lobo" Ramirez	25 year to life in prison
Carlos "Charlie Brown" Acala	10 years in prison
Bobby "Silent" Lopez	sentenced to death

Anthonio "Chuco" Guillen   25 years to life in prison

Andrew "Mad Dog" Cervantes   life in prison

Take a good long look at both of these lists mis Hermanos y Hermanas, for all of you who are caught up in the gang, declaring your honor and loyalty to the Carnales and providing your services for their personal gain, your reward may be a life in prison with those whom you idolize. Ironically many of those serving life sentences have dropped out of the gang, realizing the stupidity of la vida loca but only too late. Think about those individuals who are doing time for the Carnales. Do you think the Carnales paid for their attorneys? Do you think the Carnales and the gang are sending them money? Do you think the Carnales are taking care of their family and children for the sacrifice they supposedly committed for the righteous cause of La Raza? Well the answer to all these questions is a big, "No!" So you can continue to be a cowardly punk for the Carnales and end up dead or with a life sentance or you can grow up and learn how to count past thirteen or fourteen.

As I end this book I am scheduled to be released in twelve days, after having wasted seventeen years of my life behind walls and now having finally answered God's calling. I have put my trust in Him and wherever He leads I will follow. I have tried to "do it my way" all my life and the end results are always the same: failure! Now I want to live my life God's way.

My brothers and sisters, "Trust in the Lord with all your heart and lean not on your own understanding; in all your ways acknowledge him and he will make your paths straight" (Proverbs 3:5,6).

May God be with you and keep you all from evil and hatred and bring you to the knowledge of a new life with purpose and hope in Him.

Your brother in Christ,

Soldier of the Lord,

Willie "Shadow" Ramirez Stokes